An Overseas Parent's Guide to UK Education

by

Dr Julian Davies

Principal, Abbey College, Cambridge

Dr Martin Stephen

Former High Master, St Paul's School, London

Dr Julian Davies (Principal of Abbey College, Cambridge) is a biologist and a former research scientist at the University of Illinois. He conducted his PhD research on the effects of climate change in the Antarctic. Julian has been Principal of Abbey College since 2002, leading it to become one of the most academically successful and sought-after independent colleges in the UK. Its students have a stunning record of obtaining places at top British and world universities.

Dr Martin Stephen (former High Master of St Paul's School) was only the second person in history to have held both High Master posts in English Independent schools, at The Manchester Grammar School and St Paul's School in London. He was also Headmaster of the prestigious Perse School in Cambridge and was elected Chairman of the Headmasters' and Headmistresses' Conference (HMC), the organisation that represents leading independent schools. Martin is the author of over 20 books on education, literature and history, including the acclaimed *Educating the More Able Student: What Works and Why*, *The English Public School: A Personal and Irreverent History*, and five novels. He has travelled and lectured extensively and is a Founder Governor of the London Academy of Excellence, arguably the UK's most successful state school and a Sunday Times *Sixth Form College of the Year*, which recently achieved 26 offers from the universities of Oxford and Cambridge.

Contents

Introduction		vii
Chapter 1	The UK Education System: Examinations	1
Chapter 2	The UK Education System: Schools	19
Chapter 3	The UK Education System: Colleges	31
Chapter 4	The UK Education System: League Tables & Inspections	37
Chapter 5	The UK Education System: Universities	47
Chapter 6	How to Get In: Applying to a School or College	57
Chapter 7	How to Get In: Applying to University	93
Chapter 8	How to Avoid a Bad School or College	103
Chapter 9	What Makes an Excellent School or College?	117
Chapter 10	A Day in the Life of ...	129
Conclusion		135

Published in the United Kingdom in 2021 by
RSL Educational Ltd
www.rsleducational.co.uk

ISBN 978-1-914127-18-2

Dr Julian Davies and Dr Martin Stephen assert their right to be identified as the authors of this work.

Copyright © 2021 by Dr Julian Davies and Dr Martin Stephen

Illustrations and cover image © Shutterstock

Cover design by Raspberry Creative Type

All rights reserved. No part of this book may be reproduced, stored in or introduced into a retrieval system, or transmitted, in any form or by any means (electronic, mechanical, photo-copying, recording or otherwise), without the prior written permission of the publisher.

10 9 8 7 6 5 4 3 2 1

Also Available

For School Entrance Exams

Online resources

11 Plus Lifeline (printable resources for all subjects): **www.11pluslifeline.com**

Books

RSL Creative Writing: Book 1
RSL Creative Writing: Book 2
RSL Creative Writing: Book 3

RSL 11+ Comprehension: Book 1
RSL 11+ Comprehension: Book 2
RSL 11+ Comprehension: Multiple Choice, Book 1
RSL 11+ Comprehension: Multiple Choice, Book 2

RSL 11+ Maths
RSL 8+ to 10+ Comprehension
RSL 13+ Comprehension

For GCSE

GCSE Maths by RSL, Higher Level (9-1), Non-Calculator

GCSE Spanish by RSL, Volume 1: Listening, Speaking
GCSE Spanish by RSL, Volume 2: Reading, Writing, Translation

GCSE French by RSL, Volume 1: Listening, Speaking
GCSE French by RSL, Volume 2: Reading, Writing, Translation

GCSE German by RSL, Volume 1: Listening, Speaking
GCSE German by RSL, Volume 2: Reading, Writing, Translation

www.rsleducational.co.uk

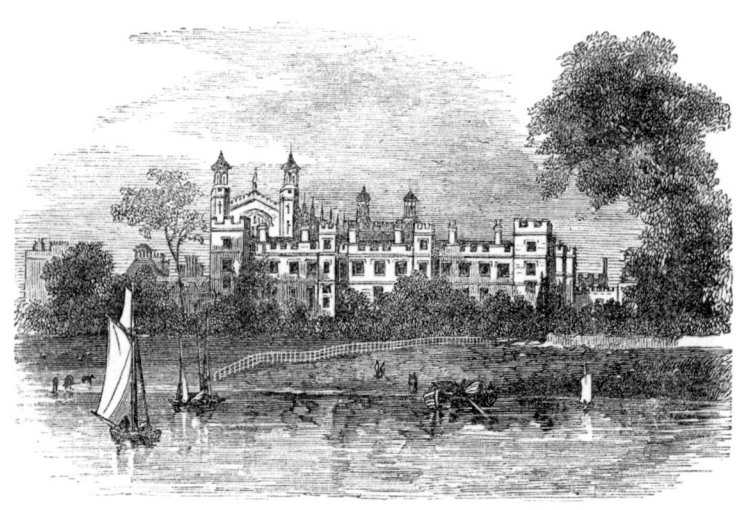

Why this book?

Many thousands of overseas parents send their children to schools and colleges in the UK every year. The initial contact procedure and choice of destination are often controlled by education agents, whose income relies heavily on the UK schools that employ them. This makes it difficult for overseas parents to obtain truly independent advice on their choice of school or college, or even on whether to choose a school or a college.

The aim of this book is to give parents accurate and factual information about the UK education sector and to help them make the best choices of school, college or university. It is a guide to the inner workings of these institutions, from two of the most respected and experienced insiders in the field.

∼

Introduction

Recent years have seen a huge increase in the number of overseas families sending their children to be educated in the United Kingdom.

The reasons are clear.

British schools achieve some of the best academic results in the world. They can offer unusually high levels of pastoral care, as well as encouraging students to participate in a wide range of activities outside the classroom.

Many schools and colleges can justifiably claim to be specialists in dealing with overseas students. Young people who attend them will usually take either A-level examinations or the International Baccalaureate, both of which are excellent and widely accepted qualifications: not only for the UK's best universities, but for the best universities in the world.

A major advantage of an education in the UK is the learning of English, which is the accepted medium of instruction in most of the world's top universities. Many overseas students who come to the UK are seeking to join the elite of graduates from universities across the world. The UK's geography and culture make it a natural pathway to Europe and the USA.

A further factor is the UK's continuing emphasis on advanced teaching of STEM subjects, in particular Maths, Biology, Chemistry and Physics. The UK's 'single science' GCSE examinations are among the strongest in the world for those who wish to specialise in these subjects, while A-levels are among the most demanding of all 18+ qualifications and as such are loved and respected by leading universities. The Further Mathematics A-level in particular is an outstanding preparation for degree-level study of Mathematics, Engineering and other science-based subjects.

Another reason for the popularity of a British education is the lasting reputation of some UK universities, of which Oxford, Cambridge, Imperial College, University College, London and the London School of Economics are probably the most sought-after for overseas candidates. These are sometimes known as the 'G5'. While schools are honest in not guaranteeing any student a place at these and similar universities, they often specialise in preparing students for entry and have a wealth of relevant experience.

So why do overseas parents and students need a book like this one?

The British education system is complex and fragmented – it confuses even people born in the UK – and there are a large number of schools and colleges to choose from.

As only one example of the confusion the system can cause to overseas parents, the word 'college' is widely used, but in fact has several different meanings. It can mean the all-important colleges of the Universities of Cambridge and Oxford, and the rather less meaningful colleges at a university such as Durham. It is often used to describe the many independent fee-paying colleges in the UK, usually (though not always) offering tuition to 16 to 18-year-old students. Yet it is also used by a number of independent *schools* – including some of the most famous in the world, such as Eton College.

To make sense of all this, in this book we use the word 'school' to describe institutions that accept children from the age of 11 or 13 and 'college' to describe fee-paying colleges that largely take overseas students from age 14 upwards. Where the difference is not important, we also sometimes use the word 'school' in a general sense, covering schools and colleges.

There is a significant difference between state schools and independent schools (sometimes called 'public schools' – see Chapter 2) and colleges, with the former usually not allowed to accept overseas students for lengthy periods of study. Judgment of a school's quality is often based either on 'league tables' or inspection reports. Which league table is the most reliable? There are two bodies that inspect schools, known as Ofsted and ISI. Which is better? What is the difference between a school ranked as 'outstanding' in an inspection and one ranked as 'good'?

UK schools are based on a different culture and philosophy from that sometimes found overseas. At its best, British education encourages students to ask questions, whereas in some parts of the world, large class sizes make asking questions a luxury. On our many visits to overseas schools, it took us a long time to realise how reluctant some students were to answer a question in class, for fear of getting the answer wrong and feeling shamed.

Teachers in the UK often have a wider-ranging relationship with their students, taking overall responsibility for their wellbeing and happiness and not just their academic progress. Perhaps most importantly, British education encourages creativity and independent thinking: one reason why it is such a good preparation for top universities. On the other hand, some overseas students feel that their role is to do what the teacher tells them to, rather than adding their own ideas and learning on their own initiative.

The best UK schools do not expect the student to work all day, but to find time for art, drama, music, sport and a range of non-academic activities. This can be worrying for those overseas parents who are more accustomed to a heavy work routine. Yet British, European and American universities know that their students will not work 24 hours a day and offer places to those who have shown they can work *and* play and that they are self-motivated, without the need to be driven by parents or teachers.

All these differences can be a source of confusion to parents seeking to choose a school or college, and to students when they arrive in the UK: as well as coping with being away from home for the first time, they often have to grapple with a new culture and ideology.

At the heart of the problem is the lack of *independent* advice. Schools and colleges produce their own brochures and DVDs, but these are obviously designed to sell their product and are the opposite of independent. Agents place many overseas students in UK schools or colleges, but the majority receive either an up-front fee or a percentage of the student's fees, in exchange for introducing them to the school. There are many honourable agents, but there will always be some who recommend the school that pays them the most, rather than one that is best for the student.

There are books published in the UK that purport to be guides to schools and colleges, but many of these charge schools for inclusion, so they obviously tend to suggest that all their paying clients are wonderful. What's more, many publications are not full or accurate guides to the schools or colleges in the market. When one of the authors of this book was High Master of St Paul's School, London, he refused to be part of any book or publication that charged the school for inclusion. Why? The reputation of the school was so great that it did not need to advertise for applicants. Indeed, there were often more applicants than the administrative system could easily cope with. The result is that many of the 'top' schools undertake no advertising or publicity for the simplest reason of all: they have no need.

The aim of this book is simple: to give a clear and factual guide to the culture and principles of UK schools and colleges, and to help parents ask the right questions when they are choosing where to send their child. We offer suggestions about how to manage an application to the UK's top institutions, as well as examples of some of the best practice in schools and colleges, which will help parents know what to look for. On the basis that many parents will wish their child to go on to a British university, there is also a section on the basic dos and don'ts when choosing universities and applying to them. Lastly, in order to make the unfamiliar world of UK education a little more familiar and friendly, we have included the chapter 'A Day in the Life of …', which shares the personal experiences of some overseas students.

Dr Julian Davies
Dr Martin Stephen

Chapter 1

The UK Education System: Examinations

A-level, International Baccalaureate, International Foundation Programme, GCSE, English Language exams, Regional differences

∼

A-level and AS-level

The final examination most commonly taken in UK schools and colleges is the A-level (short for Advanced Level), which can be combined with a one-year AS-level course. The AS-level is a qualification in its own right: it does not contribute to a pupil's A-level grade, should they take the further year needed to sit an A-level.

A-levels are usually taken at the end of a two-year course from ages 16 to 18, though they can be sat at any age. The A-level is demanding and attempts to offer both breadth and depth, which explains why it is recognised internationally and liked by the world's top universities. Most A-levels require students to sit two separate written exams, although many subjects have an additional assessment component. This may involve laboratory-based coursework for sciences, portfolios for art subjects, or tests of speaking and listening for languages.

There are around 80 A-level subjects. Some of these are more respected by universities than others. Top universities refer to 'facilitating' A-levels: those that give access to the greatest number of degree courses and are favoured by universities. Facilitating A-levels are generally agreed to be as follows:

- Biology
- Chemistry

- English Literature
- Geography
- History
- Physics
- Modern and Classical Languages
- Mathematics and Further Mathematics

Art and Music will not usually be seen as qualifying A-levels for mathematical or science subjects. Meanwhile, a university is not likely to be impressed by someone with an A* grade in their native language.

Many overseas students aspire to enter the world of business so opt for Economics A-level, but in fact this A-level is not a condition of acceptance for a degree course in Economics – even at the London School of Economics, one of the most demanding universities in the world. Not all schools offer Economics A-level, so universities are quite accustomed to students who will study the subject for the first time at university. This does not mean that Economics is a 'bad' A-level: while it may not be required, it is likely to be accepted and welcomed.

> **Warning:** A-level subjects that demand written essays, such as Economics and History, and to a certain extent even Biology, are often difficult for overseas students, many of whom find it easier to learn spoken English before they acquire advanced skills in written English.

Some degree subjects will insist that you have specific A-levels. For example, you should study *both* Biology and Chemistry if you wish to study *either* Biology or Chemistry at university. Medicine requires Chemistry (though not, interestingly, Biology). Candidates for Politics, Philosophy and Economics (PPE) at Oxford University will need Maths A-level. This poses a dilemma for some students: *Do I study the subjects I most enjoy or those I do best at, and what if these subjects are not the ones I need for my desired degree subject?*

Of course, you must choose subjects that are right for your chosen degree course, and in which you are going to get good grades. You may want to be a doctor more than anything else on earth, but you won't get a place to read Medicine at a UK university without an A* or at least an A in Chemistry and probably also in Maths or Physics.

> **Warning:** Check that your A-levels qualify you for your desired degree subject. An easy way to do this is to access **theuniguide.co.uk**, which has a special tool for this purpose.

Some A-levels are subjects that the student will already have studied at school. Others, such as Economics, can be taken up by students with no prior experience of the subject.

> **Warning:** Check with your school or college that you can take your chosen A-level without having studied the subject before, if this is your situation.

A common pattern is for students to start studying four AS-levels in their first year, then drop one of them (keeping their AS-level qualification in that subject) and carry three through to A-level. This is not obligatory: some students sit four or more A-levels. However, good universities do not demand more than three A-levels, other than a handful who prefer their candidate for Mathematics to have both Maths and Further Maths A-levels.

The AS-level examination is taken at the end of the first A-level year, and is separate: the AS result does not count towards the A-level a year later. Although AS-level does not influence the A-level result, good grades are worth having, as they are tangible proof of a student's level of achievement after the first year of A-level study. This makes them important for university applications.

A-levels are given grades A*, A, B, C, D, E and U (unclassified or fail).

The leading universities usually expect at least three A* or A grades: commonly, two A*s and one A. For a popular subject at a Russell Group university (see Chapter 5), two A* or A grades and a B grade are a normal requirement. Each university course's typical offer can be researched at **theuniguide.co.uk**, though universities' own websites are the definitive source for this information.

> **Warning:** While it is sometimes a good idea to study four A-levels (the best mathematicians often take both Further Maths and Maths A-levels, alongside two other subjects), be careful. The *number* of A-levels you sit matters far less than the *grades* you achieve. Merely increasing the number of A-levels sometimes brings the student no advantage, and it can even disadvantage them. Thus a student applying for a top university might be offered a place on the condition that they achieve three A* or A grades, but universities are quite capable of increasing this to four A* or A grades if the candidate is sitting four A-levels.

The Extended Project Qualification

The Extended Project Qualification (EPQ) is a standalone qualification that some students take at the same time as studying for their A-levels. It is a unique programme of study in which students choose their own project and develop it independently, guided by a school tutor.

Students undertake the EQP in order to study a topic in more depth than for A-level and to help them develop their skills in areas such as research, planning, synthesis and presentation. The aim is for a student to produce a final assessed piece of work, which can be an extended essay, a performance, a design or an artefact, depending on the area of study.

The work is assessed by the student's school before being certified by an English or Welsh exam board and given UCAS points, albeit at a lower tariff than allocated for A-levels. University admissions tutors view the EPQ favourably as it shows evidence of commitment to self-study and it can therefore help a student gain a university offer: while leading universities do not usually demand that the applicant takes an EPQ, it is desirable to do so.

It is important to note that students in the sixth form undertake the EPQ voluntarily, because it involves significant additional study time. This may not suit all students. In addition, not all schools or colleges offer the EPQ. Some may instead offer their own tailored extension courses for sixth form students.

The International Baccalaureate

The International Baccalaureate is administered by a non-profit organisation based in Geneva, Switzerland and founded in 1968. It offers four programmes, but the one used most commonly by overseas students is the Diploma Programme, aimed at 15 to 19-year-olds and commonly known as the IB or International Baccalaureate. In contrast to A-level, which focuses on three or four subjects that can all be, for example, sciences or languages, the IB examines students across six diverse subject areas:

- Studies in Language and Literature
- Language Acquisition
- Individuals and Societies
- Sciences
- Mathematics
- The Arts

Students study some subjects to Standard level (equivalent to AS-level), but must take three or four to Higher level (equivalent to A-level).

In addition, there is a Diploma Programme core, with three required elements:

- Theory of Knowledge (TOK)
- The Extended Essay (EE)
- Creativity, Activity, Service (CAS)

The principle of the Extended Essay has now been adopted by the A-level system, in the form of the optional EPQ (see above). Meanwhile, the Creativity, Activity, Service dimension is covered by most UK schools, but not always in the manner prescribed by the IB.

Results in the IB are awarded as an overall mark, the top obtainable score being 45. Russell Group universities (see Chapter 5) usually have a minimum mark of 34 for entry, with most courses demanding 34 to 38, while Oxford and Cambridge and highly-contested courses at other universities require 40 to 42.

In summary, the IB goes for *breadth*, while the A-level aims for *depth*. There is fierce debate over which is better, as well as which is harder. There is no easy answer. The two systems are based on different philosophies. There is a body of educational opinion that believes it is healthy for students to follow a broad range of subjects until they are 18 or 19, and the American university system carries this principle forward into undergraduate study. Equally, some students cannot wait to specialise and be rid of subjects they do not enjoy. The greater depth of study at A-level in theory allows students to spend less time at university, saving them money.

In practice, the decision between IB and A-level needs to be taken on an individual basis. Is the student an all-rounder? Do they already know what academic subjects they wish to specialise in and what subject they want to read at university? If, for example, the student is committed to reading Mathematics at university, Further Maths and Maths A-level are a brilliant combination. On the other hand, if the student is undecided, the IB has advantages.

The overseas parent needs to be aware of a number of other issues regarding this choice. Some UK schools adopted the IB not only because it was a good qualification (which it is), but because it gave them a distinct identity and a different character in the marketplace – in effect, their own 'brand'. These schools have an ideological commitment to the IB, and the parent needs to be certain that their son or daughter is being offered the IB because it is the correct qualification for them, not just because it matches the school's preferences.

In addition, it is very expensive to run both the IB and A-level, and the dilemma is that staff appointments (a school's most expensive outlay, usually taking up between 50% and 65% of its total income) have to be decided some months before it can be known how many students will sit A-level and how many IB. Late applicants need to ask whether they are being encouraged to take either A-levels or the IB because the school hasn't found enough students to fill that course.

> **Warning:** If a school encourages you to take either A-level or the IB, make sure that it is doing so for educational rather than commercial reasons.

International Foundation Programme (IFP)

The International Foundation Programme (commonly known as IFP) is a course available to overseas students as an alternative to A-level. The IFP acts as a dedicated university preparation course and, although it can enable entry to universities outside the UK, it is not globally recognised. Within the UK, it is a well-respected alternative to A-level, although at a lower academic standard.

IFP courses typically last for one academic year and so have approximately half the academic content of an A-level programme. For this reason, they are not accepted by the elite UK universities, such as Oxford and Cambridge, which do not consider IFP students to be sufficiently well prepared for their undergraduate courses. Some of the high-ranking so-called Russell Group universities (see Chapter 5) will accept a student who has sat an IFP course, but the grade required will be very high. It is uncommon for a student who has sat IFP to enter for a university course in Medicine or Dentistry or to study Engineering or Maths at a top-ranked university. However, IFP courses are widely accepted by universities ranked below the Russell Group.

> **Warning:** It is important that students who chose IFP understand that it is at a lower academic standard than A-level and that this will make entry to a top university more difficult.

Students select a specific pathway when choosing an IFP course (e.g. Business Management, Engineering or Science) and study all components within that pathway. As an example, a Business Management pathway will comprise the compulsory study of business, financial accounting, economics, mathematics and statistics. A good IFP pathway will also include modules teaching skills required at university, such as research and presentation skills. Such things are often of particular benefit to students who may not have conducted individual research or given many presentations to their class or year group. An essential component of an IFP course is the teaching of academic English. This may lead to a student sitting a separate English exam at the end of the IFP course, such as the IELTS examination.

> **Warning:** Be aware of the compulsory nature of the IFP curriculum. It is worth ensuring that it contains the subjects you hope to study, at the correct level. For example, if you are an able mathematician, you may find the depth of A-level Maths and Further Maths more rewarding than the mathematical component of an IFP course.

There is no agreed UK-wide curriculum for IFP courses and they are not created by the main A-level examination boards. Individual colleges and universities create their own courses and use external moderation and accreditation to validate student outcomes. As a result, there can be a range of academic quality between the IFP courses offered by different institutions. It can be difficult to compare the standard of these courses, so it is worth looking in detail at the university destinations achieved by students who have previously completed an institution's IFP programme. If previous IFP students have gained entry to well-respected universities, it would suggest that the IFP course is of high academic quality.

Warning: If a college or other IFP provider does not publish a *full* list of the universities that previous students have entered, ask to see one. Some institutions may only show a small, edited, selection of student destinations and this may give a misleading picture of the quality of the IFP course.

General Certificate of Secondary Education (GCSE)

Students study for the GCSE exam between the ages of 14 and 16 (school years 10 and 11). Students typically study eight to ten subjects and sit all their exams at the end of the two-year course. The GCSE is a well-known exam in the UK and is respected by employers and universities. As with the A-level exam, the government determines the academic standard and content, while exam boards that are independent of the government create, mark and award the qualification.

There are three main boards in England: OCR, AQA and Edexcel (see below). Although the boards set exam papers independently of each other, they are all considered to offer the same standard of exam, because this is regulated by the government. Employers and universities are usually only interested in the grades obtained.

The examination boards are commercial organisations that also create and sell GCSE examinations outside the UK. These exam papers are not the same as those sat within the UK and are referred to as International GCSEs (or IGCSEs) to avoid confusion with the British exams. The academic standard of IGCSE examinations is not determined by the government, but the level is usually similar to GCSEs in the same subjects. Although there is some debate among teachers as to whether the GCSE or IGCSE in any given subject is harder, there is an acceptance by employers and universities that the standards are comparable.

Students study a wide range of subjects at GCSE level, some of which are compulsory (English Language, Maths and Science), and some of which may be optional, depending on the school (e.g. students often have to choose between Geography and History). A typical GCSE programme for a UK student might include English Language, English Literature, Maths, Chemistry, Biology, Physics, History or Geography, a modern foreign language (most commonly French or Spanish), and two personal choices such as Information Technology and Economics.

Overseas students may be offered a reduced range of subjects, depending upon the student's English language proficiency. A typical programme for an overseas student would not include English Literature or a modern foreign language but might include Further Maths or Business Studies. There is also a different English Language GCSE curriculum for overseas students called English as a Second Language. As the name suggests, this course is designed around developing and assessing the English of second-language learners.

> **Warning:** GCSE courses are taught to younger students than A-level. Younger overseas students can have a lower English proficiency and it is important to be sure that a school has teachers who are skilled and experienced in this area. If a student's English level is not yet high enough to study a GCSE course, it is best to take a dedicated pre-sessional English Language course first.

GCSE uses a numerical grading system, with 9 being the highest grade and 1 the lowest.

Schools and colleges that specialise in educating overseas students may have GCSE programmes that last for the standard two years or for 18 months, or even one year. Shortened GCSE courses feature fewer subjects, typically five or six on a one-year course. A shorter course may be suitable for a student who is aged 15 or 16.

> **Warning:** It can be tempting to spend one year on a GCSE course rather than the standard two years. However, top universities have a strong preference for a greater number of GCSEs (eight to ten) than it is possible to take on a one-year course. Taking a one-year GCSE course may reduce subsequent options for entry into a top university.

The Pre-U

In 2008 a new qualification, the Pre-U, was created, intended as an alternative to A-level, offering additional depth and going beyond the standard A-level syllabus. However, too few schools opted for the new examination and it will be withdrawn in 2023. Resits for those who sat the exam in 2023 will still be available in 2024.

Exams of English proficiency

Overseas students benefit from continuing to improve their English language proficiency in UK schools, either before or during their academic studies. Pre-sessional programmes are suitable for students who have not yet achieved the required English level. These programmes typically teach students who have already reached the A2 or B1 level on the standard measure of language proficiency, the Common European Framework Reference (CEFR). A student at A2 level is considered to have an 'Elementary' level of proficiency, while B1 is referred to as 'Intermediate'.

The examinations from the Cambridge University exam board, Cambridge Assessment, have become one of the leaders in school and college English testing. The Cambridge Assessment exam, 'B1 Preliminary', is often used to test whether a student has reached B1 level. Pre-sessional courses can also teach students to reach the next level, B2, which can be tested using the Cambridge Assessment 'B2 First'.

Universities use Cambridge Assessment's International English Language Testing System (IELTS) as the standard English exam to measure the proficiency of overseas students. The test assesses the four areas of language competence: reading, writing, speaking and listening. It awards a score from 1.0 (lowest) to 9.0 (highest) in each area and also gives an overall score from 1.0 to 9.0. The IELTS level required by universities varies, but is usually around 6.5 to 7.5.

Students who have reached the required level of proficiency to study an academic programme delivered in English will benefit from ongoing English instruction to further develop their ability. Such language courses often run alongside academic programmes such as GCSE, A-level or IFP and aim to help students improve their score in the IELTS exam, in order to reach the level required by universities.

English proficiency and academic courses

CEFR level	Description	IELTS level	Academic programme suitability
C2	Proficient	9.0	
		8.5	
C1	Advanced	8.0	
		7.5	Usual lowest level for Oxbridge degree
		7.0	Lowest level for top university degree
B2	Upper intermediate	6.5	Many university degrees
		6.0	
		5.5	Lowest level suitable for A-level
B1	Intermediate	5.0	Lowest level suitable for GCSE and IFP
		4.5	Pre-sessional English
		4.0	Pre-sessional English
A2	Elementary	Below 4.0	Beginner English

The language level of overseas students is often the single biggest determining factor in their success. Improving English while in the UK is therefore extremely important.

Warning: Some students hope that they will suddenly improve their IELTS score in their final year at school in the UK, just in time to reach university level. This is rarely the case: it is difficult to increase your IELTS score above 6.0 without dedicated work over time. This should be given the same priority as academic study.

The United Kingdom: differences in schools and examinations

The name 'United Kingdom' reflects the fact that contemporary Britain is an amalgam of four geographical areas, each with a distinct national identity.

Scotland was an independent nation until the Act of Union in 1707. It retained its own legal system, and since 1999 there has been a relatively powerful Scottish Parliament in Edinburgh (see below). There is a lively debate about whether Scotland should become an independent country.

Wales was conquered by Edward I of England during the 13th century. It was incorporated into the Kingdom of England by the Laws in Wales Acts of 1535 and 1542. Despite the length of time that it has been a part of the United Kingdom, there remains a fiercely separate Welsh identity. Visitors will see bilingual road signs in English and the ancient Welsh language.

Ireland was claimed by England for many years and bitterly fought over. A series of events, including Oliver Cromwell's bloody conquest of the country (1649 to 1653), saw many English settlers take up land, particularly in the north. As a result, when most of Ireland became independent again in 1921, six counties in the north remained under English control and are known to this day as Northern Ireland, a part of the United Kingdom – unlike the Republic of Ireland, which is a completely separate country. The separation of the largely Protestant north from the largely Roman Catholic south has provoked violence for many years.

The English parliament's response to calls for independence in Scotland and Wales, and for Northern Ireland to become part of the Republic of Ireland (none of these calls have yet been endorsed by popular votes), has been to adopt a system of 'devolution'. This means that considerable powers are given to the parliaments of Scotland, Wales and Northern Ireland. These powers include education, so there are differences between schools in the various regions.

In practice, this matters little for the overseas student. Such differences as there are apply mainly to state schools, which overseas students cannot attend. While all of the UK regions have good independent schools or colleges, these will offer either A-levels or the International Baccalaureate, rather than requiring pupils to follow any local examinations. The only exception is that a small number of Scottish independent schools require students to sit Highers.

Regional differences should not affect overseas university applicants. Students can apply through the same UCAS system used by all UK universities. Scottish universities are among the oldest in the world, and universities such as Edinburgh and St Andrew's are heavily sought-after by students from across Britain.

The Scottish education system

Scotland has a slightly different educational system from the rest of the United Kingdom. The difference is seen most clearly in Highers and Advanced Highers, the rough equivalent of English AS-levels and A-levels. Students can take four or five Highers, usually in one year. Four Highers are the minimum requirement for university entry, but the highest-ranking universities are likely to ask for five.

Highers offer fewer subjects than A-level – there are 72 available, whereas for A-level there are 123 – and were originally designed for entry to Scottish universities, which tended to offer four-year courses, rather than the three-year courses common in the rest of Britain. Traditionally, Scottish students who wished to go to top English, Welsh or Northern Irish universities would add on a second year of study to take A-levels. Nowadays they can opt for Advanced Highers instead.

While broadly equivalent to A-level, Advanced Highers are sometimes seen as sightly harder: Oxford and Cambridge are reported to accept students with slightly lower grades in these exams. Students preparing for top universities would usually expect to take three Advanced Highers.

The basic Highers courses offer breadth, but not the same depth as A-level. As a result, Universities credit fewer UCAS points (see Chapter 7) to students with Highers than to those with A-levels. For example, an A grade in a Higher earns 33 points, while an A grade at A-level scores 48 points. The points awarded for Advanced Highers, on the other hand, are the same as those for A-level.

Our general advice to overseas students who want to attend a UK university is that there is no advantage to sitting Highers (although there is also little disadvantage to doing so). In any event, they are rarely (if ever) taught outside Scotland, and though they are excellent exams in their own right, they offer no additional advantage to the overseas student. By and large, Highers and Advanced Highers will only be relevant for students attending Scottish schools and wishing to go to Scottish universities.

The Welsh education system

The distinguishing feature of the Welsh educational System is its emphasis on the teaching of the Welsh language. Overseas parents need not worry about this. Independent schools and colleges in Wales usually do not insist on a knowledge of Welsh. There is no requirement for pupils to sit examinations in Welsh.

The Northern Irish education system

Northern Ireland offers no special challenges to overseas parents or pupils. Independent schools and colleges accepting overseas pupils offer substantially the same curriculum as English schools.

Regional examination boards

A possible source of confusion for overseas parents is the fact that Britain's A-level and GCSE examinations are offered by several different agencies, known as 'awarding bodies' or 'exam boards'. There are five of these:

- AQA (Assessment and Qualifications Alliance)
- CCEA (Council for the Curriculum, Examinations & Assessment) – offers exams in Northern Ireland
- OCR (Oxford, Cambridge and RSA Examinations)
- Edexcel (a brand owned by Pearson)
- WJEC (Welsh Joint Education Committee), under its WJEC and Eduqas brands

What this means in reality is that a candidate at one school or college who sits, for example, an A-level or GCSE in Chemistry may sit an exam set and marked by one exam board, while their friend at a different school or college may sit an exam in the same subject but set and marked by a different board. Candidates do not choose which board they sit. This is done by the school or college, and usually it is the teachers of a given subject who decide. Thus a student may sit exams from several different boards, depending on their subject choices.

Rumours always circulate that one or another board's exam is easier or harder, but in fact there is central authority to ensure that standards are consistent. Parents should not base their choice of school or college on its choice of exam boards: it is not a decisive factor in a pupil's success or failure.

To put it differently, it is not vital to understand and remember the information in this section!

Though the exam boards have regional roots, they now operate across wider areas. The three boards based in England – AQA, OCR and Edexcel – offer all their qualifications in England, but a smaller number in Northern Ireland (only when a qualification meets the local regulator's requirements) and in Wales, where they 'fill in the gaps' when no equivalent homegrown qualification is available. The

Wales-based WJEC offers qualifications in Wales (mostly under its WJEC brand), in England (nearly always under its Eduqas brand) and in Northern Ireland (under either brand). CCEA, despite previously offering qualifications in England and Wales, now only operates in Northern Ireland.

All exam boards offer a wide range of qualifications, though not all boards offer every qualification in every subject.

Chapter 2

The UK Education System: Schools

Types of school, History & culture, Accommodation, Language, Holidays

∼

Independent schools

Independent schools in the UK are schools that charge parents fees to educate their children. Independent schools for younger children are known as 'preparatory schools' or 'prep schools'. These educate children from around the age of 5, up to 11 or 13. In the state sector, which offers free education to every UK family, the equivalent schools are known as 'primary schools'.

Of more interest to overseas parents are the senior schools, which educate children from 11 or 13 years upwards. In the independent sector, these are sometimes known – very confusingly – as 'public schools' (see below). In the state school sector (provided free of charge to UK residents), there are various types of school, which go by a range of names but are known in general as 'secondary schools'. Whatever type of school they attend, at around the age of 14 children begin a two-year course that leads to their taking GCSE examinations in a number of subjects.

Some overseas students come to UK schools as relatively young children, but the most popular option is to come over for a two-year 'sixth form' course leading to A-level or the International Baccalaureate (see Chapter 1). This approach saves money, and the student is more mature by this age and readier to leave home. Independent colleges tend to specialise in older pupils and to treat them as young adults, while independent schools may give their sixth formers greater freedom than other students but still regard them as part of a structure that runs from age 11 or 13 to age 18.

The largest organisation representing independent schools is the ISC (Independent Schools Council), which is an umbrella organisation representing a number of different groups of independent schools. These are:

GSA (Girls' School Association) **www.gsa.uk.com**
HMC (Headmasters' & Headmistresses' Conference) **www.hmc.org.uk**
IAPS (Independent Association of Prep Schools) **iaps.uk**
ISA (Independent Schools Association) **www.isaschools.org.uk**
The Society of Heads **www.thesocietyofheads.org.uk**
AGBIS (Association of Governing Bodies of Independent Schools) **www.agbis.org.uk**
ISBA (Independent Schools' Bursars Association) **www.theisba.org.uk**

The ISC is affiliated to four other organisations:

SCIS (Scottish Council of Independent Schools) **www.scis.org.uk**
WISC (Welsh Independent Schools Council) **www.welshisc.co.uk**
BSA (Boarding Schools' Association) **www.boarding.org.uk**
COBIS (Council of British International Schools) **www.cobis.org.uk**

One of the confusing elements in UK education is that there is often a different terminology used to describe year groups in state and independent schools. Remember that in the UK only 7% of children attend fee-paying independent schools, while 93% attend free state schools. For overseas parents seeking to explore the UK educational system, any initial enquiries may lead them to the state sector, which is only available to British citizens. The terminology differs greatly. In state schools, the year groups are known by simple numbers: Years 1 to 6 for primary school children and Years 7 to 13 in secondary school.

In the following table of state school year groups, 'age in school year' refers to a student's age after their birthday during that school year:

Age in school year	Terminology	Stage
12	Year 7	Key Stage 3
13	Year 8	
14	Year 9	Key Stage 4
15	Year 10	
16	Year 11	(GCSEs for most students)
17	Year 12	
18	Year 13	(A-level for suitable students)

- At the end of each key stage, students are deemed to have reached a crucial stage in their studies and are assessed using government-administered tests.

Independent schools, on the other hand, are free not to test their students if they so wish. Even more irritating for overseas families trying to understand the UK system is that while some independent schools adopt the government terminology for year groups, others take pride in using their own descriptions, sometimes found only in that school. Thus you will find independent schools with years known as 'Remove' or even 'Shell'. Christ's Hospital school names its year groups 'Second Form' (there is no 'First Form'), 'Third Form', 'Lower Erasmus', 'Upper Fourth' (there is no 'Lower Fourth'), 'Great Erasmus', 'Deputy Grecians' and 'Grecians'. More logically, many secondary schools start the numbering of year groups from the year the child enters the school, so classes range from 1 to 7 rather than 7 to 13.

Further confusion may be added by independent schools' affection for the old-fashioned word used to describe 16 to 18-year-old students who are studying for A-level or the International Baccalaureate as the 'Sixth Form' (though you may sometimes still come across this term outside the independent sector), with the two years divided up into Lower 6th and Upper 6th. At St Paul's School, London, these are instead referred to as the 'Upper 8th' and the 'Lower 8th'.

The reason for this terminology is historical, and it has remained not for any educational reason, but simply because no-one has bothered to change it. As a general rule, the older the school, the more it will have its own language. A good hint when applying to a school is to try and find out if there are any unusual phrases used there and ask what their origin is. As an example, why does Eton College refer to a school term, of which there are three each year, as a 'half'?

One does occasionally need a sense of humour when dealing with the local language of independent schools. A popular game in some schools is known as 'fives', despite the fact that it is played by either two or four people: the reason for the name is that the ball is hit not by a racket but by the player's gloved hand, which has, of course, five fingers.

One parent was very confused when told he would be shown round by a 'polly'. A senior student arrived who bore no resemblance to a parrot ('Polly' is a popular name for parrots in the UK) and only later did the parent discover that the school in question called its *prefects* (see below) 'pollies'.

Confusion is also created by the old-fashioned word 'public schools' to refer to fee-paying independent schools. Unlike in the USA, where public schools are just that – schools that the public can attend free of charge – UK independent schools are attended by only 7% of the school population: those who can afford the high fees and pass an entrance exam. As with so much in Britain, the term 'public school' is inherited from history. Many of the more famous schools were founded in the fourteenth, fifteenth and sixteenth centuries when rich men left money to pay for the education of poor children. Hence these schools at their outset were very definitely open to the public. As time went on, the charitable endowments were lost as a result of corruption or simply the passage of time, and the once 'public' schools came to depend on those who could afford to pay the fees.

However, the term 'public school' also refers to a crucial division within the sector, between boarding and day schools. In history, the top public schools were largely boarding schools. In the 1860s, when the government launched an enquiry into the public schools, it identified nine 'great' schools of England. Only two of those schools – St Paul's in London and Merchant Taylors' School in Northwood – were day schools. The other seven – Eton, Harrow, Westminster, Winchester, Charterhouse, Shrewsbury and Rugby – were all boarding schools. The nine 'great' schools were also boys-only. The most famous girls' schools were not usually founded until late in the nineteenth or early in the twentieth century. Co-education in UK independent schools is now more common than single-sex education, but did not become widespread until the 1970s.

Boarding has declined in popularity among UK parents in recent years, partly through changes in social attitudes but also because rising fee levels have meant that fewer families can afford to pay. This has led in some schools to an increasing proportion of boarders coming from overseas. Obviously a boarding school, offering secure accommodation, 24-hour supervision and a range of weekend activities, can be seen as ideal for overseas families who have no relatives or friends in the UK with whom their child can stay while attending a high-achieving day school. On the other hand, day schools are becoming more attractive for UK parents, and many former boarding schools now only accept day pupils.

The boarding house

Many overseas parents are surprised by the importance of the boarding house a pupil is placed in. Houses can host from 30 to 80 children, who live, sleep and do their homework there. In some schools – Uppingham is one example – students even eat meals in their house. The Housemaster or Housemistress is instrumental in setting the atmosphere and culture, and has primary responsibility for a child's wellbeing.

Houses can differ greatly within the same school, some being very sporty, others being known for their music or drama, and so on. It's important for an overseas parent to realise that they have a choice of boarding house – and therefore of Housemaster or Housemistress – once a school place has been offered.

> **Warning:** If you don't like the first House or Housemaster/Housemistress to whom you are introduced, ask for another option. Base your choice on the Housemaster or Housemistress, not on the physical state of the house or where it is situated. People will influence your child's development more than buildings!

Quite a lot of overseas parents are put off a UK school if there are large numbers of other overseas students in the school or boarding house. This can be a valid concern. Young people are often not adventurous in making friends and will naturally gravitate towards people who speak their language and share their culture, whereas one of the reasons for sending your child abroad is for them to speak English and learn to mix with people from other backgrounds. But it's not quite as simple as that.

If your child is spending the whole working day in lessons where the only language is English, while every written word, every advertisement and every TV and radio announcement is in English, it can actually be helpful for them to speak their own language for an hour or so every evening. Also, some schools with a majority of non-overseas pupils have a policy to ensure that English-speaking young people talk to those with different native languages. Check whether the school has a policy for helping students of all nationalities to mix.

> **Warning:** Many boarding schools have large numbers of students go home at weekends (see Chapter 8). Before you choose a school, check how many students your son or daughter will socialise with over a normal weekend, or if the school encourages 'weekly boarders' to take overseas students home with them.

Hierarchies

It is a tradition in many independent schools to give significant responsibility to pupils. Thus there will not only be a Head Boy or Head Girl (nowadays more commonly called 'Head of School'), but also a number of prefects. While these students do not teach, they will supervise various activities and be expected to ensure good discipline in the school. They may have the power to administer minor punishments if a pupil misbehaves, though of course these will never be physical punishments: corporal punishment has long been banned in UK schools.

The overseas student who joins a boarding house will also find a senior pupil serving as House Captain (appointed by the Housemaster or Housemistress), usually with a team of prefects working under them. These prefects' duties will include ensuring that younger pupils get to bed on time and that there is good behaviour in the dormitories.

Homestay

Because of the high standards in many independent day schools, you might be tempted to lodge your child in the home of a family whom you do not know. Be careful! 'Homestay', as it is sometimes called, can work really well, but only if the host family has been checked and recommended by the school. If your child is staying with another family, it is essential that you meet them beforehand. These people will be looking after your child, and will have a huge influence on their progress.

One example: Your son or daughter comes 'home' after school, very upset. They have had an argument with a friend, or a teacher has given them a bad mark. You are thousands of miles away and even if your child can speak to you, given the difference in time zones, how can you decide whether this is a serious problem, or the sort of thing that happens every day to a child? And if you decide that it is a serious problem, what can you, all those miles away, do about it? In a good homestay, the child will be able to share their concerns with the homestay family, and that family will be able to decide if the problem needs to be reported to the school.

The homestay family will have a clear line of communication with your child's school, so they can report any problems quickly and easily to the right person. You need to trust the family to take these decisions on your behalf.

There is another reason why any homestay has to be approved by your child's school. If there are problems with a student, social or academic, the first thing a good school will do is check their accommodation arrangements. If they think these are unsatisfactory – for example if the host family are doing it simply for the money, are not there for long periods or are failing to supply a student's basic needs – they might well say that the student can only remain at the school if alternative accommodation is found.

English language

One of the authors recently addressed a group of nearly 200 15-year-old students in a major Chinese city. All of them appeared to understand his speech without needing a translator. It was a great tribute to the teaching of English in overseas schools, and he thought at the time how far across the UK one would have to go to assemble 200 students as fluent in Mandarin as those overseas students were in English.

Yet the high standard of English among overseas students can cause a sense of false security. Many UK schools will insist on an IELTS score of 6.0 before they accept an overseas student (though this varies a lot between schools and colleges), and many leading universities demand 7.5 (see Chapter 1). Nonetheless, good as IELTS exams are, they do not fully prepare a student for sixth form work. Firstly, academic teaching uses technical terms often not covered in conventional language courses. Secondly, an overseas student's home teachers will usually not have been native English speakers, and English as spoken by a native speaker is sometimes subtly and sometimes obviously different from that taught and spoken in the student's home country.

Therefore, a vital question to ask of a prospective school is whether further tuition is available in English. Many schools will assume that the overseas student will learn to be more proficient simply by living and working in an English-speaking environment. Of course, some overseas students will already be fluent, but the school should have someone to whom the overseas student can turn for help should he or she encounter any difficulties.

Parents should also ask whether the school encourages opportunities for overseas students to practise their English in public, such as by taking part in school debates.

> **Warning:** Does your school of choice offer further teaching in English to overseas students?

Holidays

Independent schools tend to have longer holidays than state schools. There is often a one or two-week 'half-term' break in the middle of the first (winter) term, in October, and a holiday of up to four weeks over Christmas and the New Year. There is a short half-term break in the second (Easter) term, followed by a three or four-week holiday at the end of this term in March/April. In the summer term there is usually a one-week half-term break, and a long, eight or nine-week holiday in July and August. These holidays can cause problems for overseas families, not least because of the expense of several flights back home every year.

It is usually not a good idea for students to stay at the school over the holidays, even if this is permitted: schools without pupils are very lonely places. One good solution is a guardian. This is an adult who will agree to be responsible for the child while they are in the UK and act on behalf of the child's parents, though if this is not a family friend it can be an expensive option.

Some schools and colleges are able to put overseas students in touch with host families for the holidays. Overseas students may even be invited to spend the holidays with a British schoolfriend – particularly if they make it known in their friendship group that they would welcome such an invitation. Staying with a UK family for Christmas can be an especially interesting experience and it is considered a great honour to be invited to do so.

Location

Many independent schools, and boarding schools in particular, are in fairly isolated settings, or near to small villages or towns. For many overseas parents, proximity to an international airport such as Heathrow or Manchester is essential.

The state sector

There are many good state schools, but by and large these are only available to UK residents. There have been some stories about people promising places in state schools as a cheap option for overseas students, but the chances of this happening are virtually non-existent, other than for short periods of time on exchanges. Good state schools are usually over-subscribed, and it would damage a school's reputation if they taught overseas students when local, tax-paying residents could not get places.

Chapter 3

The UK Education System: Colleges

Purpose & culture, Accommodation, Holidays, Course start points, University Foundation Programme

∼

Overseas students often choose to move from high school abroad to an independent college in the UK, in order to study a course such as A-level before moving to a British university. These colleges are different from other schools in that the majority do not offer education to younger students: they usually focus on pre-university courses, although some do offer GCSEs.

The term 'sixth form college' has declined in use. You will more often hear the terms 'Year 12', for the first year of the A-level programme, and 'Year 13' for the second. Some colleges offer the IFP course, which is referred to as a Year 13 programme, because it is a one-year course taken before university entrance.

What are colleges for?

In general, most colleges that educate overseas students aim to help children move from their home country's school system to the adult environment of a UK university. A good college will provide a specialised and supportive environment for this educational and cultural transition to occur in the best way for each child. Colleges approach this task in two main ways:

- By teaching pre-university courses in a way that helps students to pass exams and be ready for the challenging world of UK universities.

- By helping students to settle into life in the UK and understand British educational expectations, such as the value placed on having and sharing opinions.

British universities are held in high regard across the world and attract students from many different countries. As colleges teach mainly pre-university courses, they also tend to have a wide mix of overseas students. A key concern is to have mechanisms to encourage socialising and friendship between students of different nationalities. Such mechanisms may include such things as mixing nationalities within a boarding house or classroom and insisting that only English is spoken during lessons. A good extra-curricular and social programme will also encourage mixing between nationalities. Other effective mechanisms to break down barriers include encouraging pairs or small groups of students from different countries to work together on projects, and peer-mentoring schemes to help students learn from each other.

A college's student body tends to comprise students aged 15 to 19. This can result in colleges having a different feel to secondary schools. The students may be treated more like young adults and given greater independence. For one thing, there may well be no school uniform in a college.

Whereas a student who joins a secondary school for A-level or IFP will encounter an existing student group that may have studied together since the age of 11 or 13, an interesting feature of college life is that students who start a new A-level or IFP course will generally join at the same time, forming a new student body in the college. This creates a situation where everyone is in the same position, with the same chances. Crucially, it facilitates the rapid formation of new friendships. These friendships can make the move to the UK and to a new college easier and more enjoyable.

College teaching usually takes place in small classes: around ten students is likely to be typical. Small classes enable teachers to get to know each student and provide guidance tailored to their needs. A smaller class also allows each student to ask and answer questions in every lesson, and this helps overseas students to become more confident in voicing opinions. This is an excellent preparation for university, where this ability is highly prized.

The teachers who work at colleges have often chosen to do so out of a desire to specialise in pre-university teaching, and many also work for exam boards, marking A-level and GCSE papers during the summer holidays. This helps them to gain a deep understanding of exactly what is expected in the exams.

Many colleges place great emphasis on improving the language proficiency of their overseas students. Students with lower English proficiency can be given the option of taking a pre-sessional English course (see Chapter 1). Colleges often continue to provide additional English language lessons alongside academic courses such as A-level. Such lessons are usually designed with the demands of the IELTS exam in mind, as this is the language qualification required by UK universities.

Colleges provide a strong emphasis on helping students with university applications. This can take the form of careers guidance, advice on the right university and course, help with writing applications, and practice for university admissions interviews.

College boarding options

Students have a number of boarding options when studying at a college. The options range from living in a college boarding house, living with an approved host family or living independently of the college provision.

The most common option is for overseas students to live in college boarding accommodation. A number of colleges have accommodation at their campus and this is sometimes referred to as 'on-site boarding'. On-site boarding is a popular option as it removes the need for a student to travel to attend lessons. On-site accommodation is often provided in purpose-built, new buildings which can have a high standard of provision, such as single-occupancy study bedrooms with their own private bathrooms. Alternatively, college boarding may also be located away from the campus. This may be within walking distance, or students may need to use public transportation. Many colleges in London do not offer on-site boarding: students travel each day on London's well-served transport system.

Many colleges offer students the option of living with a host family, also known as 'homestay'. This is also offered by many schools and is discussed in Chapter 2.

Students who are over the age of 18, and therefore defined as an adult in UK law, can sometimes have the option of living in private accommodation, entirely independently of the college. This may involve living in a rented flat or sharing a house with other students. In such cases, the student is responsible for all of the arrangements, from signing a legal rental contract, to arranging and paying for utilities, such as electricity and gas.

> **Warning:** Living independently of a college can be tempting for older students but it is a big step to take. Such students must make their own living arrangements and provide themselves with all of their meals. They must also ensure that they attend lessons on time and meet all homework deadlines. This option is only suitable for students who are mature enough for these challenges. A good college will have clear rules about independent living and will only permit students to pursue this option if they have demonstrated the high level of maturity required.

College campuses vary. Some benefit from the facilities that would be expected in a school, with a full range of classrooms and laboratories, on-site boarding, sports facilities, art and music studios, dining halls providing all meals, and outside spaces for socialising and sport. Other colleges may comprise buildings with limited facilities, just for the delivery of lessons: classrooms, laboratories and libraries. Such colleges are often found in the centre of cities such as London, where students benefit from other nearby amenities such as public libraries and museums.

> **Warning:** College campuses are usually different from those at traditional English boarding schools. Boarding schools are often located in the countryside and can have considerable outside space for playing fields, grand old buildings (rather like Hogwarts from *Harry Potter*), and even their own small churches, known as chapels. Colleges are almost always far younger institutions with newer buildings, often located in cities such as London, Oxford and Cambridge.

Holidays

Colleges and schools follow the same pattern of term dates, but there can be differences in holiday arrangements. Whereas schools are more likely to ask students who cannot return home to stay with their guardian or a host family, most colleges remain open during half-term and Easter breaks, meaning that students can remain in supervised accommodation and continue to use college facilities, as well as receiving the usual meals.

All UK schools and colleges close for the summer and Christmas holidays. The majority of students return home at that time, but some colleges will offer alternative accommodation (generally not at the college boarding house) for the Christmas break. This usually involves staying with one of the college's host families.

Course start points

The majority of academic courses at UK schools, colleges and universities start in September. A number of colleges also provide alternative start points to reflect the needs of students from other education systems. For example, it is often possible to start an A-level or GCSE programme in January and follow it for 18 months: that is, for less than the standard two years.

Pre-university study 'on campus'

A number of (often) lower-ranked universities offer students the option of studying a University Foundation Programme (UFP) at their campus. Such courses are similar to IFP courses (see Chapter 1) and are usually delivered by private companies. The courses have a one-year duration and facilitate entry into the university at which they are located. Progression from the UFP course to the university's undergraduate degree depends on passing the course's exams.

> **Warning:** Because many on-campus UFP programmes are provided at lower-ranked universities, it can be difficult to move to a more prestigious university, such as a member of the Russell Group, after such a programme.

> **Warning:** A UFP provides education in the adult environment of a university. Students on such courses may not always benefit from the same degree of pastoral care and support (see Chapter 9) found in a school or college environment.

Chapter 4

The UK Education System: League Tables & Inspections

School league tables

One of the main influences on parental choice for overseas students are the league tables. These give details of the results achieved by schools and are usually published in descending order, with the best at the top.

League tables are a relatively recent concept. They were invented by a journalist in the 1980s. He had heard two heads of independent schools bragging about their results, and realised that only very rarely did schools make these public. In August, when the A-level results came out, he rang a number of the schools with the best reputations and asked them for their actual A-level results, then published them as a league table, based on the percentage of A-levels achieved at A or B grade. The results were surprising, with some well-known schools doing quite badly and some relatively unknown schools doing very well. There are now many league tables, often produced to wildly different specifications.

One simple problem is that the results for state schools in the UK are released a week earlier than those for independent schools. The overseas parent who thinks they have obtained a 'league table of UK schools' needs to check whether this is a table of state schools, independent schools, or both. State school feature less prominently at the top of mixed league tables than do independent schools.

Another potential cause of confusion is that there are not only separate league tables for state and independent schools, but for A-levels and GCSEs.

League tables can be very misleading in other respects. Many of the top schools and colleges only accept very bright, high-achieving students, so the high grades these students achieve are hardly surprising. Where a school is only admitting pupils whose intelligence puts them in the top 5% of their age group, it would be surprising if they did *not* do well.

> **Warning:** Ask questions of any league table you are shown. On what is it based? A* and A grades? Grades A* to B? A* to C? A* to E (E is the basic pass grade)? Ask whether all schools and colleges have been included in the league table, or only those who submitted their results to the publisher.

The situation nowadays can be even more unhelpful to overseas parents:

1. While travelling we have been shown league tables ranking schools that we simply did not recognise as bearing any resemblance to reality. We do not know where these league tables came from or what evidence they were based on.

2. Some years ago a group of the most successful independent schools decided not to make their results available for the purpose of media league tables. Therefore, many of the most famous schools do not appear, at least in the early league tables after exam results are announced. One result of this is that less successful schools can achieve artificially high rankings.

3. Very slight differences in results can make a dramatic difference to a school's standing. Some league tables have to show results to two decimal places in order to distinguish between schools.

4. League tables record *all* results, rather than results by subject.

Many schools have some subject departments that achieve excellent results and other departments that do less well. It is no use to a child who wishes to read Chemistry at university if their school as a whole achieves over 90% of A-levels at A* or A, but Chemistry results are nearer to 70%.

> **Warning:** Find out a school's results in the subjects your child wishes to study, as well as their overall results. Ask whether the school has a list of results achieved by overseas students.

5. Remember that it's not your child's exam results, in themselves, that decide whether or not it was worthwhile to send them to the UK: it's what these results allow them to achieve afterwards. Ask about the *destinations* of the pupils who have left the school over the past three years. Are pupils succeeding in getting to the type of university you want your child to go to? Are students reading (studying) the same university subjects that your child wishes to read? Remember that some degree courses are far harder to get into than others, so check how many of the school's pupils go on to read highly competitive subjects such as Medicine, Law, Veterinary Science and Economics, and how many go to Oxford and Cambridge.

6. Schools with a weak 'tail' of students tend to do badly in league tables, yet they often offer a brilliant education to more able children. Some schools have a mixed ability entry, with some very clever students but others who are less academic. Some are particularly good at working with children who have special educational needs (SEN), and these students will often not achieve the highest grades. These schools may be doing a brilliant job, helping the more able achieve A*s while also helping other students to get the all-important C grade.

7. Very few schools publish the results achieved by overseas students separately, yet these statistics would be particularly in-

teresting for overseas parents. Even if a school does not publish this information, it is worth asking whether they have any sense of how their overseas students perform in comparison to others in the school.

8. It is not only the overall results of a school that decide the individual child's happiness and success there.

   Parents need to explore whether schools provide extra 'catch-up' help in academic subjects that overseas students may have started later in their school careers than their British (or indeed European) counterparts. This can be relevant for subjects such as Biology, Chemistry and Physics. It will be no consolation to an overseas parent if the school in general is doing well, but overseas students are struggling because their earlier schooling has failed to cover work that other students have completed.

> **Warning:** Check whether your selected school offers extra provision in your child's chosen subjects, to cover anything that they might not have studied previously.

9. There is no hierarchy that human beings will not try to exploit, and league tables are no exception. In the early days there used to be two ways of trying to gain a higher ranking. An obvious one was to only allow pupils into the sixth form who had achieved excellent grades at GCSE and who seemed destined to get A or at least B grades at A-level. Thus parents found that the school their child had attended for up to five years rejected them for the final, crucial phase of their education. An extension of this in schools and colleges was to expel pupils who did not, after one year of the two-year A-level course, show signs of being likely to gain an A or B grade. (See the section on 'culling' in Chapter 8.)

   A second way to push the league tables in one's favour was to have two 'streams' of A-level candidates – those who were clearly going to get top grades, and those who were not – and put those who were not going to achieve top grades into a unit that, for league table purposes, counted as a different school.

Both these practices have been challenged, legally and morally, but if independent schools make it clear in writing that any pupil who does not reach certain standards by a certain time may be asked to leave, the parents and the student have little comeback.

It is easier for a college to constitute part of itself as a different entity than it is for a school, but for example it is theoretically possible for an independent school to treat an overseas boarding house as a separate school, so that its results are reported separately. The chances of a fee-paying school attempting to cheat the league tables are slim – independent education in the UK is stringently regulated, inspected and reported on – but the risks are there, and overseas parents need to be aware of them.

> **Warning:** Check that your child will not be asked to leave after GCSEs (or after the first year of A-level) if their progress falters, and check that the league table results that attracted you to the school or college in the first place are those achieved by *all* the students enrolled, not just the high achievers. The only way to do this is by asking the school or college.

Probably the most reliable league table is the one published annually by the Sunday Times newspaper, towards the end of November. This is recommended because it contains results from all independent schools and colleges listed with the Independent Schools Council (ISC) and has a range of data. In particular, it takes into account both A-level and GCSE results. This is important, because for young people who are in UK secondary education from the age of 11 or 13, GCSE results may be as important as A-levels in deciding their future. It also reveals schools that welcome a large number of clever new students at sixth-form level, artificially boosting their results.

University league tables

League tables ranking universities are now as common as those ranking schools. Indeed, for many years before UK schools were ranked there were league tables of world universities, largely based on their research output. There were also the unofficial league tables ranking Oxford and Cambridge colleges on the degree results achieved by their students: the Norrington (Oxford) table from around 1962 and the Tompkins (Cambridge) table from 1981, named after their supposed creators. The statistical method adopted by the Tompkins Table is seen as more accurate than that for Norrington, and Tompkins is now accepted as the standard for both universities.

The new university league tables are as confusing as those for schools, if not more so. This is because they contain a number of elements, including such things as entry standards, student satisfaction, quality of research, graduate employment prospects and the number of First Class degrees awarded.

University league tables are problematic, because what employers think of a university is arguably more important for a student's career than, say, levels of student satisfaction whilst at the university. They are also hampered by the fact that different departments and courses within the same university can differ greatly in standard. It is entirely possible for a university with one of the most admired Engineering departments in the world to have a near-disastrous Biology department, for example.

There is a simple rule for judging the quality of a course at a given university: look at the standard offers it makes (for example on **uniguide.co.uk**). The higher the offer (see Chapter 7), the greater the demand for that degree: a clear indication that the department offering the course is popular and successful.

Another important metric in university league tables is the percentage of graduates who are in full-time employment within a year of graduating. It is sometimes difficult to explain to students that the most important thing in choosing a degree course is not whether the *student* likes the course; it is whether *employers* like it and recruit people from that university with that degree. Graduate employment figures do not tell the full story – there is often no way of knowing whether the graduate in employment is working for a top law firm or flipping hamburgers – but they are a helpful pointer to the most important function of a degree, which is arguably to get the graduate a job.

League tables and colleges

There are few leagues tables that show a ranking of all UK independent colleges and none are published by authoritative sources such as the Sunday Times. Some colleges do appear in the main school league tables, but many do not.

When placed in a league table, colleges are often ranked on the percentage of A-levels graded A* and A. Such ranking tends to be misleading, as some colleges are academically selective and only admit students with the very highest grades at GCSE. These colleges are therefore likely to be placed higher than others.

> **Warning:** You may wish to check whether or not a college is academically selective. A high-ranked non-selective college may be adding a great deal of value for students, whereas a lower-ranked selective college (or school) may be underperforming.

Some colleges encourage overseas students to follow an IFP instead of an A-level course, and this can influence their ranking in a league table based on A-level results. For example, a college may only allow a small number of their most able overseas students to take the A-level programme, with the rest following IFP. Such a college may be placed high in a league table despite having very few, and only the strongest, overseas students sitting A-level.

As IFP courses are so varied in academic standard, there are no college league tables based on IFP results.

> **Warning:** Look at a college's website or brochure for details of the number of A-level students that sit exams each year. If the number is small, or not published, it may indicate that most students in that college follow an IFP programme and only a small number of able students are permitted to sit A-levels. This leads to an artificially high college ranking based on A-level results and doesn't relate to its performance in IFP – the main work of such colleges.

It is possible to take A-level exams that test proficiency in a foreign language such as Arabic, Chinese, Russian or a European language. The exams are created for non-native speakers to be tested on their progress in learning a new language. Overseas students may take the A-level in their native language and will often obtain a high grade when doing so. However, university admissions staff are aware that this happens and may give less credit to the exam result than they would to the result from a non-native speaker. A college that has many overseas students sitting their native language A-level may be placed unfairly high in league tables.

Inspections

State schools in England are inspected and reported on by Ofsted (the Office for Standards in Education). Inspections take place approximately every four years and schools are ranked as 'outstanding', 'good', 'in need of improvement' or 'inadequate'.

Independent schools in England can opt to be inspected by Ofsted, but the majority choose to be inspected by ISI, the Independent Schools Inspectorate. Unlike Ofsted, ISI does not make a single overarching judgement on a school but instead reports on various aspects of its provision, grading each one as 'excellent', 'good', 'sound' or 'unsatisfactory'. The areas inspected include pupils' achievement, the curriculum, teaching, pupils' personal development, pastoral care, welfare, health and safety, and governance, leadership and management. Boarding schools are inspected more frequently than day schools and there is an additional set of standards for boarding pupils' welfare. ISI is validated by Ofsted and the UK government, and though the style of inspections differs somewhat, the basic standards used by Ofsted and ISI are the same.

Schools have to publish their inspection reports on their websites, but reports can also be accessed through Ofsted and ISI.

All schools in Scotland are inspected by Education Scotland (**education.gov.scot**), and in Wales by Estyn (**www.estyn.gov.wales**). Boarding schools in Wales are also inspected by Care Inspectorate Wales (**careinspectorate.wales**). Schools in Northern Ireland are inspected by ETI (the Education and Training Inspectorate): **www.etini.gov.uk**.

It is very difficult to describe the difference between 'excellent' and 'good', not least because the judgement is influenced by an inspector's personal point of view. The best advice to parents is to welcome an 'excellent' rating, but never to reject a school because it is only classed as 'good'.

Inspection reports are very useful, but schools can change rapidly, and it is always worth noting the date of the last inspection. Also, a school's most recent report may be of the Regulatory Compliance type, which checks that the school or college meets the minimum standards set out in law and has rather less information than fuller Educational Quality reports.

Chapter 5

The UK Education System: Universities

Oxford & Cambridge, The Russell Group, Accommodation, Degree results, 'New' universities

The UK university system has a simple basic truth: the better the university or course, the harder it is to get into. You also need to be aware that universities in the UK operate a very different system from those in the USA. In America, students tend to start on a general course, then specialise in a 'major' course. In the UK, students apply for what would in the USA be a 'major' or specialist subject, following this from the start and throughout their three or four-year course. The British system is better for students who already know what they want to study or 'major' in.

> **Warning:** You will be invited to attend many educational 'fairs' or exhibitions, at which the majority of exhibitors will be universities. Bear in mind that many of the best universities are not represented at these events, for which the exhibitors pay a lot of money. In particular, beware of any institution at the fair that offers a guaranteed place. You should not choose a university, school or college because it offers you a place quickly: you should choose it because it is the best for you.

Remember that the student is choosing a *course* to study as much as a university. It is entirely possible for one subject to be outstanding at a particular university, while another subject there is mediocre.

How do you judge? Try to find out the 'graduate prospects' for each subject (see Chapter 4). Just as you choose a school in order to get a place at a good university, so you go to that university to get a job or research position – so find out how many graduates in that subject in that university gained jobs in the year after they left, and how many are still unemployed. As a very rough guide, at least 80% should be in work.

Oxford and Cambridge

Oxford and Cambridge are the most desirable universities in the UK, and among the most respected in the world. As a result, they are some of the hardest to get into.

The University of Oxford is the oldest in the English-speaking world, and the world's second-oldest university in continual existence. No one knows quite when it was founded, but the first records suggest that teaching was already taking place there in 1089. In a thousand years of existence, it has accumulated 54 Nobel Prize winners and 28 Prime Ministers of the UK.

A group of academics fled from Oxford to found the University of Cambridge in 1209, as the result of a dispute with local townspeople. So far Cambridge has amassed 110 Nobel Laureates and 14 Prime Ministers of the UK. It is also famous for being the home of the academics who found the structure of DNA (the 'double helix') and of Stephen Hawking, the famous scientist, among many, many others.

Often known as 'Oxbridge', these two universities have educated many of the elite in British and world society – scientists, authors, actors, politicians and leaders across most branches of human endeavour.

As well as being difficult to get into, Oxford and Cambridge are different from nearly all other universities in the UK and across the world. They have their own entry system, which – though a part of

UCAS (see Chapter 7) – has extra demands, but the major feature to note about them is that they operate through *colleges*. Colleges are at the heart of Oxford and Cambridge, both academically and socially.

What is an Oxford or Cambridge college?

There are 31 colleges in Cambridge, 39 in Oxford. They date back to the foundation of the universities, when groups of scholars came together to found small academic communities that provided food and lodging. Colleges vary in size, the largest having over a thousand undergraduate and postgraduate students, but many having around 500. Some colleges are very wealthy, others less so. There are no all-male colleges, but a handful remain female-only. Some are ancient (University College, Oxford, was founded in 1249, and Peterhouse, Cambridge was founded in 1284), and some modern (Robinson College, Cambridge was founded in 1977, Kellogg College, Oxford, in 1990). Some are in the centre of town, others on the outskirts.

Annual league tables are produced, ranking the various colleges on the basis of students' results in final examinations. Some colleges have long-standing reputations for academic excellence, and thus are often perceived as more difficult to get into. Others have reputations for excellence in particular spheres. As an example, the choir of King's College, Cambridge, is internationally famous, and the college's Festival of Nine Lessons and Carols is broadcast around the world every Christmas.

Students apply to a college, rather than to the university. They eat in college, live in rooms either in the college or owned by it, and stay as members of the college for their whole time at university. At least some of their teaching will come from 'fellows' (sometimes known as 'dons') who are affiliated to the college, and much student sport is played in college teams.

A jewel in the crown of Oxbridge and one of its distinguishing features is the tutorial system. This involves undergraduates being taught by college fellows, and occasionally by doctoral or post-doctoral students, in groups of one, two or three students, on a weekly basis. Known as 'tutorials' at Oxford and 'supervisions' at Cambridge, these sessions are at the heart of an Oxbridge education, although there are also lectures, seminars and practicals that students have to attend. Students not only have to prepare work for their tutorials, but be prepared to discuss and, if necessary, defend it to the other students and their tutor or supervisor. Good tutorials challenge, stimulate and provoke thought about the student's subject in a way that perhaps no other system can equal.

Oxford and Cambridge are beautiful cities, and also quite small. Oxford is the larger of the two and home to another, 'new' university (see below), Oxford Brookes. It has a slightly more urban feel than Cambridge. Cambridge also has a 'new' university, Anglia Ruskin. The relatively small size of the two cities means that a student's social life is dominated by the university, whereas the London student has access to the widest possible range of clubs and activities.

There are no easy answers for the student wishing to choose between Oxbridge and a university in a big city. Yes, Oxford and Cambridge are based in small cities, but a large proportion of their population is formed by young people, and highly intelligent ones at that. This in itself creates an exciting atmosphere. Yes, both cities are an easy hour from London – but what's the point of going to Oxford or Cambridge if you are going to spend much of your time in London?

Russell Group universities

There are 24 Russell Group universities:

- University of Birmingham
- University of Bristol

- University of Cambridge
- Cardiff University
- Durham University
- University of Edinburgh
- University of Exeter
- University of Glasgow
- Imperial College London
- King's College London
- University of Leeds
- University of Liverpool
- London School of Economics & Political Science
- University of Manchester
- Newcastle University
- University of Nottingham
- University of Oxford
- Queen Mary, University of London
- Queen's University Belfast
- University of Sheffield
- University of Southampton
- University College London
- University of Warwick
- University of York

The name 'Russell Group' comes from the fact that the original 17 members used to hold informal meetings in the Russell Hotel in London's Russell Square. Their reason for joining together in 1994 was primarily to act as a lobby group for universities with a major commitment to research. The group is generally recognised as comprising some of the best universities in the UK. 60% of doctorates in the UK are given by Russell Group universities, which receive two-thirds of all research grants. 30% of all students in the UK from outside the European Union attend Russell Group universities.

Sometimes the universities founded long after Oxford and Cambridge are known as 'red brick universities'. This is because they mostly had their origins in the nineteenth century (although they were often not granted full university status until as late as the 1930s), and as a result were built of red brick, rather than the stone typical of Oxford and Cambridge. There is a debate over which university was the first to receive the title 'red brick', the battle being between the University of Liverpool and the University of Birmingham. What was different about these universities was that by and large they did not adopt the college system of Oxford and Cambridge, and that they usually had no religious element in their foundation.

There are a number of things that can confuse the overseas parent and student.

Firstly, though the 24 Russell Group universities tend to be seen as the 'best' UK universities after Oxford and Cambridge, there are some well-regarded universities that are not members of the Russell Group. These include:

- Aberdeen
- Aston
- Bath
- Cardiff
- Dundee
- East Anglia (UEA)
- Exeter
- Heriot Watt
- Keele
- Lancaster
- Leicester
- Loughborough
- Queen's Belfast
- Reading
- Royal Holloway (University of London)
- SOAS (University of London)
- Stirling

- Strathclyde
- Surrey
- Sussex
- Swansea

Secondly, the Scottish universities were founded between 1400 and 1600 under a different system from that of England. Two of them are in the Russell Group, but several, including the outstanding University of St Andrew's and University of Aberdeen, are not.

Thirdly, there is an over-arching University of London. Even though this nominally has 'colleges', including Imperial College, King's College and University College, these behave in every respect as separate universities. In fact, the use of the term 'college' is misleading here: the London university colleges have little or no resemblance to the colleges of Oxford or Cambridge.

Fourthly, the University of Durham has its own form of collegiate structure, but it is different from both Oxford and Cambridge and the London University system. For one thing, teaching is generally not carried out within colleges.

Finally, Oxford and Cambridge are very different from 'red brick' universities, but are still members of the Russell Group because they are united in their devotion to research. This reflects one of the other major divisions in UK higher education: that between 'research' universities and 'teaching' universities.

> **Warning:** Be aware that some excellent universities are not members of the Russell Group.

Living Accommodation

Students at universities other than Oxford, Cambridge and Durham are usually offered the opportunity to stay in Halls of Residence in their first year. These are expensive, and paid in addition to any tuition fees, but provide a room, heat, electricity and some meals. They are, in effect, student hostels. In their second, third and potentially fourth year a majority of students will move out to live with friends in a rented house. The standard of this accommodation can vary greatly.

Degree results

Degrees results are usually categorised as follows:

- 1st, or First Class degree
- 2:1, or Upper Second
- 2:2, or Lower Second
- 3rd, or Third
- Pass

An 'Honours' degree (for which many scientists have to study for four years) is a degree marked at anything from a 1st to a 3rd, whereas a 'Pass' merely earns an 'Ordinary' degree. A 2:1 degree is most common, although the number of Firsts awarded has risen steeply since the introduction of tuition fees for all students in 1998. There is much debate over the degree classification system, and it may change.

Historical note

There have been three major periods of expansion in university education since the formation of the universities of Oxford and Cambridge. The first came when Scotland established its universities between 1400 and 1600. The second came with a major expansion from the mid-nineteenth century that saw the establishment of a red brick university in most of England's leading cities. The third period started in 1992, with the foundation of the 'new' universities.

The 'new' universities

The first 33 new universities were founded as a result of changes made in 1992 to what had been known as 'polytechnics'. These were a type of tertiary college, designed to combine some of the theoretical aspects of a conventional university degree with practical experience. They were focused on preparing students for the world of work. From 1992 onwards, 33 polytechnics converted themselves to universities, the difference between them and the older universities being that the new institutions were designed for teaching undergraduates and could not offer research or postgraduate degrees. Since then, at least 46 new universities have been founded, in addition to the 33 former Polytechnics.

In a recent global ranking of those universities less than 50 years old, only two UK institutions came in the top 100 – Brighton and Sussex Medical School and Plymouth University. This is actually rather unfair and shows the danger of relying on league tables. It is certainly true that many of the newer universities are easier to get into, and that employers do not always regard a degree from a new university as having the same value as one from an older university. However, the new universities do offer some excellent courses.

Sometimes the newer universities gain popularity with students because they are in the same towns or cities as older, more established universities, meaning that there is a large student population. Older people often sneer at this as a reason for choosing a university, but young people enjoy each other's company and for some a large and vibrant population of intelligent people is a huge recommendation. Even though people are not meant to say it, being in the same city as a prestigious Russell Group university also adds glamour and attractiveness to a new university. Oxford Brookes University and Cambridge's Anglia Ruskin University profit from this, as do Manchester Metropolitan University, Liverpool John Moores, Coventry (next door to Warwick) and Nottingham Trent, though all have high

Chapter 5 - The UK Education System: Universities

standards in their own right.

It also needs to be remembered that a top place in the world university rankings still depends primarily on research results, which disadvantages many of the teaching-focused new universities. If the student is seeking actual employment in, for example, retail management or fashion design, a new university may actually offer a more productive path.

Chapter 6

How to Get In: Applying to a School or College

How to apply, Choosing a school or college, Types of school & college, List of leading schools & colleges

∽

Applying to an independent school

There is no single agency or office that administers applications to independent schools. Occasionally parents mistake the ISC (the Independent Schools Council) for such an agency, but they will simply direct you to apply to the individual school. Instead, you need to access the relevant school's website, which will guide you through its admissions procedures.

The majority of schools will have an admissions office that deals with applicants, or a registrar who fulfils the same function. Schools will expect you to fill out an application form, which may be online or in written format. They may require a financial deposit to secure the application, which is likely to be non-returnable if you choose not to send your child to that school. This is to discourage parents from making applications to many schools, thereby wasting the time of the ones they don't really want. The best advice is to narrow your choice of schools down to no more than five. Don't apply to a school just to find out whether you like it: apply because you've already decided that you do.

Good schools will require a reference from the child's current school. Make sure that your child's current school knows where you are applying to and supports the application. They will probably also require the child to sit some type of test or examination. In some cases this will not be an entrance test, the results of which will decide whether a child is offered a place, but a means of finding out what stage the child is at in their studies. This will ensure that they are placed in the most suitable class, form or set. Schools will tell you on their website what tests they expect a child to take.

Many of the most sought-after schools will also expect to interview the child. The interview is often used partly as a means of testing the child's command of English. Try not to prepare the child for the questions they will be asked. Firstly, it is almost impossible to guess what most of these will be. Secondly, the school wants answers that clearly come from the child, not from their parents, teachers or tutors.

Exceptions to this are standard questions such as 'Why do you want to go to school in the UK?', 'Why do you want to come to this school?' and 'What are your favourite subjects and why do you like them?' By all means prepare your child for the fact that they might be asked these common questions – but let them work out their own answers! What *is* essential is that the child has spent time going through the school's website, so they can identify the features that make that particular school different. Remember that the interviewer will not be looking for 'right' or 'wrong' answers. They want to see a young person's mind working, not that they can repeat pre-programmed answers. Encourage your child to develop their answers with examples from their own experience or from things that they have read.

If at all possible, visit the school with your child. This will not only help you and your child to decide where to apply: it will also show the school that you are a committed parent.

Remember one very important thing: the child has to be as enthusiastic about the school as their parents are. What's more, it's essential that undue pressure is not placed on a child to secure a place at a given school. Research has shown that excess pressure can cause lasting damage to a young person.

In particular, it is essential that a child does not think their parents' love is conditional upon their securing a place. The best response to an understandably nervous 11-year-old being taken to an interview by his father came when the child asked 'What will you do if I get in?' 'Why,' said the father, 'I'll give you a big hug and take you fishing.' A few minutes later the second question came. 'What will you do if I fail to get in?' 'Why,' said the father, 'I'll give you a big hug and take you fishing.'

Ten things to do when applying to a school

1. Always check that the school you are applying to could accept your child. Does it teach children of the right age and gender?

2. Does the school allow you to register when you want to? Some schools restrict entry using a waiting list, meaning that you may have to register your child years ahead. In general, the older the child, the later you can apply – but even sixth form places are usually offered as early as November, for entry in September of the following year. *Check that you can still register your child.*

3. Does the school have minimum entry qualifications, such as an IELTS English language level?

4. Check that the school will definitely offer the A-level subjects your child wants to take. This does not just mean checking that the school offers a specific A-level: it means checking that the subject will still be on offer if only a handful of pupils wish to take it, and also that your son or daughter has any qualifications (such as the equivalent GCSE) that the school requires for that subject.

5. Check that extra language tuition will be offered to students

Chapter 6 - How to Get In: Applying to a School or College

who are not fluent in English.

6. If it is a boarding school, check what happens to overseas students at weekends, when many British students may go home. If it is a day school, make sure that you have researched homestay options. Do you have arrangements in place for school holidays?

7. Check whether your chosen school offers advice on applying to American and other overseas universities, as well as to UK universities.

8. Get a copy of the school's most recent inspection report, which will come from one of two sources: Ofsted or the ISI (Independent Schools Inspectorate).

9. Check that you can afford the fees. This means asking for the actual gross amount you will be charged each term. Watch out for extras: additional fees for accommodation, books, trips … the list can be a long one.

10. Always apply to a number of different schools. You can never guarantee that you will gain a place at any one of them.

Choosing a school

What is a 'top' UK independent school? For overseas candidates, it is usually one that appears at the top of the academic league tables. As with a university, the better its performance and the higher its position in the league tables, the harder a school is to get into. However, remember that two key criteria dictate whether or not a school can be considered for a particular candidate.

Firstly, there is gender. Most independent schools are co-educational, but a number of the highest achievers are either all-boy (Eton, Radley, Harrow, St Paul's) or all-girl (St Paul's School for Girls,

Wycombe Abbey, North London Collegiate School). A further complicating factor is that a number of previously all-boys schools now take girls in the sixth form (Westminster is the best-known example, and Winchester will soon follow).

Secondly, some schools offer boarding accommodation, while many others are 'day' schools – pupils arrive at school in the morning and go back home in the evening. Some schools have both boarding and day pupils. For more information on these differences, see Chapter 2.

What are the leading schools in these categories? This is a difficult question to answer, not least because school staff can change quite frequently, and because results can vary significantly from year to year. A good head or principal can make a school, but a bad one can break it.

The list later in this chapter is not intended as a guide to the *quality* of any individual school, but to its *type*. The aim is to help parents find a school that fits their needs, based on whether it is a day or boarding school and whether it accepts girls, boys or both.

Any list, including ours, needs to be treated with caution. Some schools close, and new ones are established. Some see their reputations rise over a comparatively short space of time, while others fall. The fact that a school is not listed here does not mean that it fails to do an excellent job for its overseas students.

All the schools are secondary schools, taking pupils from the age of 11 or 13. The list is alphabetical.

A list of independent colleges follows later in the chapter.

For-profit and charity schools

The great majority of UK independent schools are registered as charities. This gives the schools various tax advantages and means that any profit must go back to the school. In other words, if a school is a charity, no-one other than paid staff will earn money from it.

However, there are also a number of 'for-profit' organisations that own and run schools and expect to make money from them. Many of these companies also have schools overseas. Education can be like any other business, offering a service to customers and making money.

Some would argue that a great strength of charitable UK independent schools is that parents' fees go back into the education their children receive, rather than lining the pockets of an entrepreneur. On the other side of the argument, a for-profit school is directly answerable to its customers and has to ensure that its product is what they want to buy. For-profit companies can also afford to use money made elsewhere to subsidise schools that have fallen on hard times.

Some for-profit schools will be omitted from the list below, not necessarily because of any weakness on their part but because not all for-profit schools are members of the Independent Schools Council (ISC), the umbrella organisation for most independent schools in the UK. Membership of the ISC is a measure of quality: if a school is not a member, it is worth asking them why. The list below is largely restricted to ISC members.

The majority of *colleges* (discussed later in this chapter) are for-profit organisations.

Single Sex, co-ed and the 'diamond' system

Schools marked with ◊ use the 'diamond' system of co-education, in which boys and girls attend the same school but are taught separately in some age groups, usually between the ages of 13 and 16.

Religious affiliation

Many UK schools were originally founded as Christian or religious institutions in which the teaching of Christianity, in its various forms, was seen as an important part of the school's culture and philosophy. For some schools that religious link remains important. For others, it is now less important, whilst in some cases it has lapsed completely.

If a school declares a religious affiliation, it is worth checking with the school what the child's involvement with that religion will be. At the highest level of commitment, does the school expect the child to belong to a particular faith? Or will the child merely be expected to attend the occasional religious service? Levels of commitment to religious observance will vary greatly from school to school, and the only way to find out is to ask the school itself.

Where a school states that it is non-denominational or uses the phrase 'all faiths', it usually means that children with any religious beliefs or none are equally welcome. Such schools commonly hold separate assemblies in the mornings for the most common religions or faiths, as well as an assembly for non-believers.

It's important not to be put off just because a schools lists itself as 'Christian', 'Church of England', 'Anglican', or as belonging to any other denomination or religion. The truth is that many schools list a faith or religious belief more out of respect for their history than out of any desire to convert children.

As a general rule, children at Roman Catholic schools are more likely to find that religious faith impacts on their life in the school. The same can apply in the case of Jewish and Muslim schools. That being said, an extract from the website of one Catholic school reads, '[We are] a Catholic foundation, but we welcome pupils of all denominations and none.' This is a common attitude.

Groups of schools and/or colleges

A number of organisations in the UK are responsible for more than one school and/or college. The main ones are:

- **ACS International**, a for-profit provider.
- **Alpha Plus**, a for-profit provider.
- **Cognita**, one of the largest for-profit providers.
- **GDST** stands for The Girls' Day School Trust. It was founded in 1872 by an Anglican (Church of England) priest, with the belief that girls should be entitled to the same quality of education as their brothers. It now numbers 25 schools.
- **Dukes Education**, a for-profit provider.
- **GEMS**, an international for-profit provider based in Dubai, which has recently taken over the Bellevue Group of for-profit schools.
- **The Harpur Trust** schools, a charity set up in 1566 to support the people of Bedford.
- **Inspired Education**, a for-profit provider.
- **OneSchool Global UK** is a charity with 23 campuses across England, many of them not present on this list because they have fewer than 200 pupils.
- **Livery Companies**. A number of independent schools were founded by a member of a London livery company, often hundreds of years ago. These organisations regulated and supported many of the trades and professions practised in the city, and sometimes became very wealthy. Nowadays several survive as organisations that donate money to good causes. The nature of the link between the company and the school varies in

each case. Some schools are supported by livery companies but do not bear the company name, and livery companies support state as well as independent schools. The livery companies that support the most independent schools are the Mercers' Company, whose schools do not bear the company's name, the Haberdashers' Company and the Merchant Taylors' Company.

- **The Woodard Corporation** is a group of Church of England schools founded by an Anglican clergymen, the first of which opened in 1848. As well as its own independent schools, it has a number of affiliated schools in the independent and state sectors.

Notes on the list of schools

Schools with fewer than 200 pupils are not included on this list. An exception has been made for specialist music and performing arts schools. Schools that came in the top 50 in a recent A-level league table, or the top 15 for IB (because there are fewer IB schools), are marked with a ✋ symbol.

Where the location of a school appears in a name, as in 'The Manchester Grammar School', no further mention is made of its geographical location. Otherwise, the nearest town or city is given.

As mentioned above, schools marked with ◊ use the 'diamond' system of co-education.

Boys' boarding-only schools

Eton College, Windsor. Church of England. ✋
- The most famous school in England. One of the nine 'great public schools of England', as named in the Clarendon Commission of 1864. 11th in a recent A-level and GCSE league table.

Harrow School, London. Church of England.
- Eton and Harrow are commonly linked as the two leading 'great' public

Chapter 6 - How to Get In: Applying to a School or College

schools in England. This is slightly surprising, in that Eton regularly out-performs Harrow at A-level. One of the nine 'great public schools of England'.
Radley College, Abingdon. Church of England.

Girls' boarding-only schools

Benenden School, Cranbrook. Church of England.
Jaamiatul Imaam Muhammad Zakaria, Clayton. Islamic.

Co-educational boarding schools

Bradfield College. Church of England.
- 19th= in a recent IB league table.

EF Academy, Torbay. All faiths.
- A school aimed at international students, or UK pupils wishing for an international-style education.

Marlborough College. Church of England.
- Founded in 1843, it was the first boys' boarding school to accept girls into its 6th form, and is now a thriving co-educational boarding school.

The Royal Ballet School, London. All faiths.
- Entry based on dance skill and potential, rather than academic ability.

Uppingham School. Church of England.
- One of the most famous British headmasters was Edward Thring, Headmaster of Uppingham from 1853 to 1887.

Winchester College. Church of England.
- One of the oldest English public schools and an intellectual hotbed. 32nd in a recent A-level and GCSE league table, but this may be misleadingly low as the school favoured the Pre-U examination. One of the nine 'great public schools of England'. Will let girls into its 6th form as day pupils from 2022, and as boarders from 2024.

Boarding and day boys' schools

Abingdon School. Interdenominational.
- 44th in a recent A-level and GCSE league table.

Bedford School. Church of England. A Harpur Trust School.
Institute of Islamic Education, Dewsbury. Islamic.
Loughborough Grammar School. Christian.
Merchiston Castle School, Edinburgh. All faiths.

More House School, Farnham. Roman Catholic.

Sherborne School. Church of England.
- Famous among other things as the school of Alan Turing, the mathematician, computer scientist and code-breaker whose work helped the Allies win the Second World War.

St Paul's School, London. All faiths. A Mercers' Company School. ✋
- One of the nine 'great public schools of England'. An academic high-achiever. 9th in a recent A-level and GCSE league table.

Tonbridge School. Church of England. ✋
- One of the few schools to have always combined boarding and day pupils, and a high-achieving school. 34th in a recent A-level and GCSE league table.

Warwick School. Church of England.

Whitgift School, Croydon. Church of England. ✋
- 5th= in a recent IB league table, 39th in a recent A-level and GCSE league table.

Boarding and day girls' schools

Badminton School, Bristol. All faiths.

Cheltenham Ladies' College. Christian. ✋
- One of the most famous girls' schools. 11th in a recent IB league table, 31st in a recent A-level and GCSE league table.

Downe House School, Thatcham. Church of England.

Godolphin School, Salisbury. Church of England.

Headington School, Oxford. Christian.

Heathfield School, Ascot. Christian.

Jersey College for Girls. All faiths.

Leweston School, Sherborne. Roman Catholic.

Malvern St James Girls' School. All faiths.

Marymount London. Roman Catholic. ✋
- 12th = in a recent IB league table.

Mayfield School. Roman Catholic.

Prior's Field, Godalming. All faiths.

Queen Anne's School, Caversham. Church of England/Interdenominational.

Queen Margaret's School, York. All faiths.

Queenswood, Hatfield. Methodist.

Roedean School, Brighton. Church of England.
- One of the most famous girls' schools.

Chapter 6 - How to Get In: Applying to a School or College

Royal High School, Bath, GDST. Non-denominational. ✋
- 14th= in a recent IB league table.

Rye St Antony School, Oxford. Roman Catholic.
St Catherine's, Bramley. Church of England.
St Francis College, Letchworth. Christian.
St George's School, Ascot. Christian.
St Mary's School, Ascot. Roman Catholic. ✋
- 8th in a recent A-level and GCSE league table.

St Mary's School, Calne. Church of England.
St Mary's School, Cambridge. Roman Catholic.
St Swithun's School, Winchester. Anglican.
- One of the most famous girls' schools.

St Teresa's, Effingham. Dorking. Roman Catholic.
Sherborne Girls. Church of England.
Talbot Heath School, Bournemouth. Church of England.
Truro High School for Girls. Church of England.
Tudor Hall School, Banbury. Church of England.
Victoria College, Belfast. Non-denominational.
Woldingham School. Roman Catholic.
Wycombe Abbey School, High Wycombe. Church of England. ✋
- An academically very high-achieving girls' school, primarily boarding. 5th in a recent A-level and GCSE league table.

Boarding and day co-educational schools

Abbot's Hill School, Hemel Hempstead. Christian.
- Lists itself as having 'some boys'.

Abbotsholme School, Uttoxeter. Church of England.
Ackworth School, Pontefract. Quaker.
ACS Cobham International School, Cobham. Non-denominational.
- 25th= in a recent IB league table.

Albyn School, Aberdeen. All faiths.
Aldenham School, Elstree. Church of England.
Ampleforth College, York. Roman Catholic.
- A famous Roman Catholic school.

Ardingly College, Haywards Heath. Church of England. A Woodard School. ✋
- 8th in a recent IB league table.

Boarding and day co-educational schools

Ashford School. Interdenominational.
Ashville College, Harrogate. Methodist.
Barnard Castle School. Interdenominational.
Battle Abbey School, Battle. Church of England/Interdenominational.
Bedales School, Petersfield. All faiths.
- A famously innovative school with a liberal philosophy.

Bede's Senior School, Hailsham. All faiths.
Bedstone College, Bucknell. Church of England.
Beechwood School, Tunbridge Wells. Non-denominational.
Belmont School, Dorking. Christian.
Berkhamsted School. Church of England. ◊
Bethany School, Cranbrook. Church of England.
Bishop's Stortford College. Non-denominational.
Bloxham School, Banbury. Church of England. A Woodard school.
Blundell's School, Tiverton. Anglican.
Bootham School, York. Quaker.
Boundary Oak School, Fareham. Non-denominational.
- Finishes at age 16.

Box Hill School, Dorking. All faiths.
Bredon School, Bushey. All faiths.
- Specialist dyslexia provision.

Brentwood School. Church of England.
Brighton College. Church of England. ✋
- A school that has pushed itself into the top 20 in the past fifteen years. 3rd in a recent A-level and GCSE league table.

Bromsgrove School. Anglican. ✋
- 9th in a recent IB league table.

Bruton School for Girls. Christian.
- Lists as having 'some boys'.

Bryanston School, Blandford. Church of England.
Buckswood School, Hastings. Non-denominational.
Burgess Hill Girls' School.
- Lists itself as having 'some boys'.

Campbell College, Belfast. Non-denominational.
- Lists itself as having 'some girls'.

Canford School, Wimborne. Christian.
Caterham School. United Reformed Church.

Chapter 6 - How to Get In: Applying to a School or College

Charterhouse, Godalming. Church of England.
- One of the nine 'great public schools of England'. Co-ed 6th Form.

Chase Grammar School, Cannock. All faiths.
Cheltenham College. Church of England.
Chetham's School of Music, Manchester. All faiths.
- An internationally acclaimed school for musicians.

Chigwell School. Church of England.
Christ's College, Brecon.
Christ's Hospital School, Horsham. Church of England.
- Perhaps the most famous charitable school in the UK where the fees are based on an assessment of parental income.

City of London Freeman's School. All faiths.
Clayesmore School, Blandford. Church of England.
Clifton College, Bristol. Christian.
- The setting for a famous poem, 'Vitai Lampada', by one of its old boys, Sir Henry Newbolt.

Concord College, Shrewsbury. Non-denominational.
Cranleigh School. Church of England.
Culford School, Bury St Edmunds. Methodist.
Cundall Manor School, York. All faiths.
Dauntsey's School, Devizes. Christian. Linked with The Mercers' Company.
Dean Close School, Cheltenham. Christian.
Denstone College, Uttoxeter. Church of England. A Woodard school.
Dollar Academy. All faiths.
Dover College. Church of England.
Downside School. Roman Catholic.
Dulwich College. Church of England.
- A wealthy and famous old school in south London, with its own art gallery. Lists itself as having 'some girls'.

Durham School. Church of England.
Eastbourne College. Church of England.
Earlscliffe School.
- Ages 15-18 only.

Ellesmere College. Church of England. A Woodard school.
Ellesmere Balllet School.
Eltham College, London. Interdenominational.
- Co-educational sixth form. 30th in a recent A-level and GCSE league table.

Embley School, Romsey. All faiths.

Epsom College. Church of England.
- Founded by doctors, the school now prepares students for all careers.

Farlington School, Horsham. Christian. A GEMS school.

Farringtons School, Chislehurst. Methodist.

Felsted School. Church of England.
- 29th= in a recent IB league table.

Fettes College, Edinburgh. Interdenominational.
- The school attended by the UK's former Prime Minister, Tony Blair. 14th= in a recent IB league table.

Finborough School, Stowmarket. All Faith's.

Framlingham College. Church of England/Interdenominational.

Frensham Heights, Farnham. Non-denominational.
- Founded in 1925 as part of a movement for progressive education, and still very progressive.

Fulneck School, Leeds. Moravian.

Fyling Hall School, Whitby. Interdenominational.

Giggleswick School, Settle. Church of England.

Glenalmond College, Perth. Church of Scotland.

Gordonstoun, Elgin. Non-denominational.
- Famous for having HRH The Duke of Edinburgh and HRH Prince Charles as former pupils.

Greenfields Independent Day & Boarding School, Forest Row. Non-denominational.

Gresham's School, Holt. Church of England.
- One of the greatest twentieth century English poets, W. H. Auden, was a pupil at Gresham's.

Haberdashers' Monmouth Schools. Church in Wales. Supported by the Haberdashers' Livery Company. ◇

Haileybury College, Hertford. Church of England. ✋
- Clement Attlee (the post-war Prime Minister) was a Haileybury pupil. The school is situated in beautiful buildings that once housed the College of the East India Company. 12th= in a recent IB league table.

The Hammond, Chester. All faiths.
- Specialises in the performing arts.

Harrogate Ladies' College. Church of England.
- One of the relatively few famous girls' schools in the north of England. Lists itself on the ISC website as having 'some boys'.

Hereford Cathedral School. Church of England.
Hurstpierpoint College, Hassocks. Church of England. A Woodard school.
Hurtwood House School, Dorking. Non-denominational.
Ipswich High School. Non-denominational. ◊
Ipswich School. Anglican.
Kent College, Pembury. Methodist.
- Lists itself as having 'some boys'.

Kilgraston School, Perth. Roman Catholic.
Kimbolton School. Church of England.
King Edward's, Witley. Non-denominational.
- Offers IB as well as A-level.

King Williams College, Isle of Man. Church of England.
Kingham Hill School, Chipping Norton. Christian.
King's College, Taunton. Church of England. A Woodard school.
King's Ely. Church of England/Interdenominational.
King's School Bruton. Church of England.
King's School, Canterbury.
- A very famous old public school.

King's School, Rochester. Church of England. An associated school of the Woodard group.
Kingsley School, Bideford. Non-denominational.
Kingswood School, Bath. Methodist.
Kirkham Grammar School. All faiths.
Lancing College. Church of England. A Woodard school.
- Lancing has one of the most impressive chapels in the UK.

Langley, Norwich. All faiths.
Leighton Park School, Reading. Quaker.
Lewiston School, Sherborne. Roman Catholic. ◊
The Leys School, Cambridge. Methodist.
Lime House School, Carlisle. Non-denominational.
Lincoln Minster School. Christian.
Llandovery College. Church in Wales.
Lomond School, Helensburgh. All faiths.
Longridge Towers School, Berwick-upon-Tweed. Non-denominational.
Lord Wandsworth College, Hook. Non-denominational.
Loretto School, Musselburgh. Ecumenical.

Boarding and day co-educational schools

Loughborough Amherst School. Roman Catholic.
Luckley House School, Wokingham. Christian.
Lucton School, Leominster. Christian.
LVS Ascot. All faiths.
Malvern College. Anglican.
- 19th= in a recent IB league table.

The Mary Erskine School, Edinburgh. Non-denominational.
- Co-ed 6th Form.

Mill Hill School, London. Non-denominational.
Millfield School, Street. All faiths.
Milton Abbey School, Blandford Forum. Church of England.
Monckton Combe School, Bath. Christian.
Moreton Hall, Oswestry. Non-denominational.
Mount Kelly, Tavistock. Christian.
Mount St Mary's, Sheffield. Roman Catholic.
Moyle's Court School, Ringwood. Church of England.
Myddelton College, Denbigh. All faiths.
New Hall School, Chelmsford. Roman Catholic.
Oakham School. Church of England.
- One of the first independent boarding and day schools in the UK to become co-educational. 17th in a recent IB league table.

Ockbrook School, Derby. Moravian.
The Oratory School, Reading. Roman Catholic.
Oswestry School. Church of England.
Oundle School. Church of England. Linked with The Grocers' Livery Company.
- Famous for one of its greatest heads, Frederick William Sanderson, who (among other things) helped to pioneer what we would now call Design Technology.

Padworth College, Reading. All faiths.
Pangbourne College, Reading. Christian.
Plymouth College. Christian.
Pocklington School. Christian.
Princess Helena College, Hitchin. Christian.
Prior Park College, Bath. Roman Catholic.
The Purcell School for Young Musicians, Bushey. Non-denominational.
Queen's College, Taunton. Methodist.

Chapter 6 - How to Get In: Applying to a School or College

Queen Ethelburga's College, York. Non-denominational. ✋
- 47th in a recent A-level league table.

Queen Mary's School. Thirsk

Queens' College, Taunton

Ratcliffe College, Leicester. Roman Catholic.

Read School, Selby. Church of England.

Reddam House Berkshire. Non-denominational. A member of the Inspired Education for-profit providers.

Reed's School, Cobham. Church of England.

Rendcomb College, Cirencester. Church of England.

Repton School. Church of England.

Rishworth School, Sowerby Bridge. All faiths.

Rochester Independent College. Non-denominational. A Dukes Education for-profit school.

Rockport, County Down. Non-denominational.

Rookwood School, Andover. Christian.

Rossall School, Fleetwood. Church of England.
- 29th= in a recent IB league table.

The Royal Ballet School, London. Non-denominational.

The Royal Masonic School for Girls. Non-denominational.
- Listed as having 'some boys'.

The Royal School, Armagh. All faiths.

The Royal School, Haslemere. Church of England.

Royal Hospital School, Ipswich. Church of England.

Royal Russell School, Croydon. Church of England.

The Royal School, Dungannon. All faiths.

Rugby School. Church of England.
- One of the nine 'great public schools of England'. Widely known through the book, *Tom Brown's Schooldays*, first published in 1857, and because of Thomas Arnold, perhaps the most famous head of a British school.

Ruthin School. Non-denominational. ✋
- 45th in a recent A-level and GCSE league table.

Rydal Penrhos School. Methodist.

Ryde School, Isle of Wight. Christian.

Rye St Antony School, Oxford. Roman Catholic.

St Anselm's School, Bakewell. Non-denominational.

St Christopher's School, Letchworth. Non-denominational.

St Clare's, Oxford. Non-denominational. ✋
- 14th in a recent IB league table.

St David's College, Llandudno. Non-denominational.
St Edmund's College, Ware. Roman Catholic.
St Edmunds School, Canterbury. Church of England.
St Edmund's School, Hindhead. Church of England.
St Edward's School, Oxford. Church of England.
St Francis College, Letchworth Garden City. Christian.
St George's School for Girls, Edinburgh. Non-denominational.
- Listed as having 'some boys'.

St James School, Grimsby. Church of England.
St John's College, Southsea. Christian.
St John's School, Leatherhead. Church of England.
St Joseph's College, Ipswich. Christian.
St Lawrence College, Ramsgate. Church of England.
St Leonard's, St Andrews. All faiths.
St Margaret's, Bushey. Church of England/Interdenominational.
St Michael's School, Llanelli. Non-denominational.
St Peter's School, York. Church of England.
- Claims to be the fourth oldest school in the world, founded in 627 AD.

Saint Felix School, Southwold. Non-denominational.
Scarborough College. All faiths.
Seaford College. Church of England.
Sedbergh School, Cumbria. Church of England.
Sevenoaks School. All faiths. ✋
- One of the leading International Baccalaureate schools. 4th in a recent IB league table. 18th in a recent A-level and GCSE league table.

Shebbear College, Devon. Methodist.
Sherfield School. Non-denominational. A GEMS\Bellevue for-profit school.
Shiplake College. Church of England.
- Co-ed 6th Form.

Shrewsbury School. Church of England.
- One of the nine 'great public schools of England'.

Sibford School, Banbury. Quaker.
Sidcot School. Quaker.
Stamford High School. Christian.
- Co-ed 6th Form.

Chapter 6 - How to Get In: Applying to a School or College

Stamford School. Christian.
- Co-ed 6th Form

Stephen Perse Foundation, Cambridge. Non-denominational.
- Originally The Perse Girls' School.

Stewart's Melville College, Edinburgh. Non-denominational.
- Co-ed 6th form.

Stoke College, Sudbury. Non-denominational.

Stonar, Melksham. Non-denominational.

Stonyhurst College. Roman Catholic.
- A famous Roman Catholic school. 19th= in a recent IB league table.

Stover School, Newton Abbot. Church of England.

Stowe School. Church of England.
- Features in David Niven's autobiography *The Moon's a Balloon*.

Strathallan School, Perth. All faiths.

Sutton Valence School, Maidstone. Church of England.

Sylvia Young Theatre School, London. Non-denominational.
- A famous theatre school.

TASIS The American School in England, Egham. Non-denominational.
- 25th= in a recent IB league table.

Taunton Senior School. Church of England.
- 19th= in a recent IB league table.

Tettenhall College. Christian.

Thetford Grammar School. Non-denominational.

Thornton College, Milton Keynes. Roman Catholic.
- Listed as having 'some boys'.

Trent College, Nottingham. Church of England.

Tring Park School for the Performing Arts. Church of England/interdenominational.

Trinity School, Teignmouth. Roman Catholic/Church of England.

Truro School. Methodist.

Warminster School. Christian.

Wellington College. Church of England.
- Named after one of Britain's most famous military commanders, the Duke of Wellington. Now a leading school, 5th= in the recent IB league table.

Wellington School, Somerset. Church of England.

Wells Cathedral School, Church of England.

West Buckland School, Barnstaple. Church of England.

Westbourne School, Penarth. All faiths.

Westminster School, London. Anglican. ✋
- One of the nine 'great public schools of England'. 14th in a recent A-level and GCSE league table. Co-educational 6th form.

Westonbirt School, Tetbury. Church of England.

Windermere School. All faiths.

Wisbech Grammar School. Church of England/Interdenominational.

Woodbridge School. Church of England.

Woodhouse Grove School, Apperley Bridge. Methodist.

Worksop College. Church of England. A Woodard school.

Worth School, Crawley. Roman Catholic/Christian.

Wrekin College, Telford. Church of England/Interdenominational.

Wycliffe College, Stonehouse. Christian.

The Yehudi Menuin School, Cobham. All faiths.
- A distinguished school for young musicians.

Day co-educational schools

Abbot's Hill School, Hemel Hempstead. Christian.

ACS Egham International School, Egham. Non-denominational. An ACS international school.

ACS Hillingdon International School, Hillingdon. Non-denominational. An ACS international school.

Akeley Wood School, Buckingham. Non-denominational. A Cognita school.

AKS Lytham. Non-denominational.
- The result of a merger of two schools in 2013, and run by United Learning, a not-for-profit group.

Alleyn's School, London. Church of England. ✋
- 49th in a recent A-level league table.

Alton School. Roman Catholic.

Argyle House School, Sunderland. Non-denominational.

Arnold Lodge School, Leamington Spa. All faiths.

The Arts Educational School London. All faiths

Austin Friars, Carlisle. Roman Catholic/interdenominational.

Babington House School, Chislehurst. Non-denominational.

Bablake School, Coventry. Church of England.

Ballard School, New Milton. Christian.

Bancroft's School, Woodford Green. Church of England.

Chapter 6 - How to Get In: Applying to a School or College

Bedford Modern School. Interdenominational. A Harpur Trust School.
Beech Hall School, Macclesfield. Non-denominational.
Belfast Royal Academy. Non-denominational.
Birkdale School, Sheffield. Christian.
- One of a small number of prep schools that decided successfully to expand to senior school level.

Birkenhead School, Wirral. Church of England.
Bishop Challoner School, Bromley. Roman Catholic.
Blanchelande College, Guernsey. Roman Catholic.
Bolton School Girls' Division. Non-denominational.
- Listed as having 'some boys'.

Bowbrook House School, Pershore. All faiths.
Bradford Grammar School. Non-denominational.
Brampton College, Hendon. All faiths.
Bridgewater School, Manchester. Non-denominational.
Bristol Grammar School. Non-denominational.
Bury Grammar School. Non-denominational. ◊
The Cathedral School, Llandaff. Christian. A Woodard School.
Cheadle Hulme School, Cheadle. All faiths.
- A school which has a long-standing tradition of co-education, unlike many UK independent schools, which are comparatively new converts.

Churcher's College, Petersfield. All faiths.
Claire's Court, Maidenhead. Christian. ◊
Claremont Fan Court School, Esher. Non-denominational.
Clifton High School, Bristol. Non-denominational.
Cokethorpe School, Witney. Roman Catholic/Church of England.
Colchester High School. All faiths. A Cognita school.
- Finishes at age 16.

Coleraine Grammar School. All faiths.
Colfe's School, London. Church of England.
Colston's School, Bristol. All faiths.
- Colston's was founded by Edward Colston, some of whose wealth was acquired in the slave trade. The school is considering whether or not to change its name.

Cranford House School, Wallingford. Christian.
Cransley School, Northwich. All faiths.
Dame Allan's Senior Schools, Newcastle-upon-Tyne. Church of England. ◊

Derby Grammar School. Church of England.
- Co-ed 6th Form.

Derby High School. Church of England.

Ditcham Park School, Petersfield. Non-denominational.

Dixie Grammar School, Market Bosworth. Non-denominational.

Downsend School, Leatherhead. All faiths. A Cognita school.
- Finishes at age 16.

Duke of Kent School, Ewhurst. All faiths.

Dunnotar School, Reigate. All faiths.

Dwight School, London. All faiths.
- 25th= in a recent IB league table.

Ecole Jeannine Manual, London. Non-denominational.
- An international French bilingual school.

The Edinburgh Academy. Non-denominational.

Elizabeth College, Guernsey. Church of England.
- Described as having 'some girls'.

Eltham College, London. Interdenominational.

Emanuel School, London. Christian.

Ewell Castle School, Epsom. Church of England.

Exeter School. Church of England.

Forest School, London. Church of England.

Gad's Hill School, Rochester. Non-denominational.

Gateways School, Leeds. All faiths.

George Heriot's School, Edinburgh. All faiths.

George Watson's College, Edinburgh. All faiths.

The Glasgow Academy. All faiths.

Gosfield School. All faiths.

The Grammar School at Leeds. Non-denominational. ◊

The Grange School, Northwich. Christian.
- One of the newly-founded co-educational independent schools in the UK, and very successful.

The Gregg School, Southampton. All faiths.

Halliford School, Shepperton. All faiths.
- Co-ed 6th Form.

Hampstead Fine Arts College, London. All faiths. A Dukes Education school.

Hampton Court House, London. All faiths. A Dukes Education school.

Heathside School, London. All faiths. A Dukes Education school.

- Finishes at age 16.

Highgate School, London. Church of England. ✋
- A rising star, which has become a leading school in recent years. 25th in a recent A-level and GCSE league table.

High School of Dundee. Non-denominational.

The High School of Glasgow. Non-denominational.

Highclare School, Birmingham. All faiths.

Hill House School, Doncaster. All faiths.

Hipperhome Grammar School, Halifax. Church of England.

Holme Grange, Wokingham. Church of England.

Howell's School, Llandaff. GDST. Non-denominational.
- Co-ed 6th Form.

Huddersfield Grammar School. All faiths. A Cognita school.
- Finishes at age 16.

Hull Collegiate School. Church of England/Interdenominational.

Hutchesons' Grammar School, Glasgow. All faiths.

Hydesville Tower School, Walsall. A Cognita school.
- Finishes at age 16.

Hymers College, Hull. All faiths.

Ibstock Place School, London. Non-denominational.

Immanual College, Bushey. Jewish.

Instituto Espanol Canada Blanch, London. All faiths.
- A Spanish Government school offering the Spanish national curriculum.

Kelvinside Academy, Glasgow. All faiths.

Kew House School, London. Non-denominational.

The King Alfred School, London. Non-denominational.

The King Fahad Academy, London. Islamic.

The King's School, Chester. Church of England.

The King's School, Eastleigh. Christian.

The King's School, Macclesfield. Church of England.

The King's School Witney. Christian.

The King's School, Worcester. Church of England.

King's College, Wimbledon (co-educational sixth form). Church of England. ✋
- Going from strength to strength. 1st in a recent IB league table, 4th in a recent A-level and GCSE league table.

King Edward's, Bath. Non-denominational.

King Edward VI School, Southampton. Non-denominational.

King Henry V111 School, Coventry. Christian.
Kings Monkton School, Cardiff. Non-denominational.
King's School, Gloucester. Church of England.
The Kingsley School, Royal Leamington Spa. All faiths.
Kingston Grammar School. Non-denominational.
Knightsbridge School, London. All faiths. A Dukes Education school.
- Finishes at age 16.

Latymer Upper School, London. Non-denominational. ✋
- 27th in a recent A-level and GCSE league table.

Leicester Grammar School. Christian.
- A very successful new foundation.

Lewes Old Grammar School. All faiths.
Lichfield Cathedral School. Church of England.
Lingfield College. Christian.
Long Close School, Slough. All faiths. A Cognita school.
- Finishes at age 16.

Lyceé International de Londres Winston Churchill, London. Non-denominational.
- A bi-lingual school offering either the French or the International Baccalaureate.

Magdalen College School, Oxford. Church of England. ✋
- A consistent presence at the top of the league tables in recent years. Co-ed 6th form. 6th in a recent A-level and GCSE league table.

Manor House School, Bookham. Church of England.
- Described as having 'some boys'.

The Marist School, Ascot. Roman Catholic.
Mayville High School, Southsea. Christian.
Meoncross School, Fareham. Christian.
- A Cognita school, one of the largest for-profit providers in the UK. Finishes at age 16.

Merchant Taylors', Crosby. Non-denominational.
- Part of the 'family' of Merchant Taylors' schools, described as having 'some boys'.

Morrison's Academy, Crieff. Non-denominational.
Mount House School, Barnet. All faiths.
Newcastle-under-Lyme School. Non-denominational.
Normanhurst School, London. Interdenominational.
North Bridge House Schools. All faiths.

- Two Cognita schools, one of the largest for-profit providers in the UK. The Hampstead school is 11-16, the Canonbury school 11-18.

Nottingham High School
- Co-educational sixth form.

Norwich School. Church of England.

Notttingham High School. Non-denominational.

Oakhill, Whalley. Roman Catholic.

Old Palace of John Whitgift School, Croydon. Church of England.

Olldham Hulme Grammar School. Non-denominational. ◊

OneSchool Global UK Hindhead Campus. Christian.

OneSchool Global UK Maidstone Campus. Christian.

OneSchool Global UK Ridgeway Campus. Christian.

OneSchool Global UK Salisbury Campus. Christian.

Our Lady of Sion School, Worthing. All faiths.

Our Lady's Abingdon School. Roman Catholic.

Parkside School, Cobham. Church of England.
- Described as having 'some girls'.

The Perse School, Cambridge. Church of England/Interdenominational. ✋
- Cambridge's oldest secondary school and a consistent high achiever in the league tables. 19th= in a recent A-level and GCSE league table.

The Peterborough School. Church of England.

Pitsford School. Christian.

Portland Place School, London. All faiths. An Alpha Plus school.

The Portsmouth Grammar School. Non-denominational.

Princethorpe College, Rugby. Roman Catholic.

Priory School, Birmingham. Roman Catholic.

The Purcell School for Young Musicians, Watford. Non-denominational.
- A highly-regarded music school.

Queen Elizabeth's Hospital, Bristol. Christian.

Quinton House School, Upton. All faiths. A Cognita school.

Radnor House, London. Non-denominational. A Dukes Education school.

Radnor House, Sevenoaks. All faiths.

Reading Blue Coat School. Church of England.
- Co-ed 6th Form.

Red House School, Stockton-on-Tees. Christian.

Reigate Grammar School. All faiths. ✋
- 48th in a recent A-level and GCSE league table.

Robert Gordon's College, Aberdeen. Non-denominational.
Rougement School, Newport. Non-denominational.
The Royal Grammar School, Newcastle. All faiths.
- One of the outstanding schools in the north-east of England.

RGS (Royal Grammar School) Worcester. Non-denominational.
Rushmoor School, Bedford. All faiths.
- Described as having 'some girls'.

Saint Nicholas School, Old Harlow. All faiths.
Salesian College, Farnborough. Roman Catholic.
St Alban's School. All faiths.
St Aloysius College, Glasgow. Roman Catholic.
St Andrew's School, Bedford. All faiths.
- Described as having 'some boys'.

St Augustine's Priory, London. Roman Catholic.
St Bede's College, Manchester. Roman Catholic.
St Benedict's School, London. Roman Catholic.
St Clare's School, Porthcawl. Non-denominational. A Cognita school.
St Columba's College, St Alban's. Roman Catholic.
St Columba's School, Inverclyde. Non-denominational.
St Dominic's Grammar School, Brewood. Non-denominational.
St Dunstan's College, Catford. Church of England.
St Edward's Senior and Sixth Form, Cheltenham. Roman Catholic.
St Gabriel's School, Newbury. Roman Catholic/Christian.
St George's College, Weybridge. Roman Catholic.
St George's School Edgbaston. Christian.
St John's College, Cardiff. Roman Catholic.
St John's School Billericay. All faiths.
St Joseph's School, Launceston. Interdominational.
St Mary's College, Crosby. Roman Catholic.
St Mary's School, Colchester. Non-denominational.
St Nicholas' School, Fleet. Church of England.
- Described as having 'some boys'.

Sancton Wood School, Cambridge. Christian. A Dukes Education school.
Scarisbrick Hall, Ormskirk. All faiths.
Southbank International School. A Cognita school.
- 18th in a recent IB league table.

Sheffield High School for Girls GDST. Non-denominational.

Chapter 6 - How to Get In: Applying to a School or College

- Described as having 'some boys'.

Sherrarswood School, Welwyn. All faiths.
Shoreham College. Christian.
Shrewsbury High School GDST. All faiths.

- Described as having 'some boys'.

Silcoates School, Wakefield. United Reformed Church.
Solihull School. Church of England.
Stafford Grammar School. All faiths.
Stockport Grammar School. Non-denominational.
Sylvia Young Theatre School, London. Non-denominational.

- A school specialising in the performing arts.

Teeside High School, Durham. Non-denominational.
Thorpe Hall School, Southend-on-Sea. Non-denominational.
Tower College, Merseyside. Christian.
Trinity, Croydon (co-ed sixth form). Church of England. ✋

- 50th in a recent A-level league table.

University College School, London. Non-denominational. ✋

- 'UCS' was one of the first independent schools founded with no religious affiliation. Co-educational 6th form. 22nd in a recent A-level and GCSE league table.

The Webber School, Milton Keynes. All faiths. A GEMS/Bellevue school.

- For children up to 16 years-old.

Wellingborough School. Church of England.
Westbourne School, Sheffield. Interdenominational.

- Finishes at age 16. One of a small number of prep schools that decided to expand to senior school level.

Westholme School, Blackburn. Christian.
Wolverhampton Grammar School. All faiths.
Yarm School. Christian.

- Founded in 1978, Yarm School has rapidly achieved an excellent reputation.

The Yehudi Menuhin School, Cobham. All faiths.

- A highly-regarded music school.

Boys' day schools

Bolton School Boys' Division. Non-denominational.
The Cedars School, Croydon. Roman Catholic.
City of London School for Boys. All faiths. ✋

- 15th in a recent A-level and GCSE league table.

Haberdashers' Aske's Boys' School, Elstree. Christian. ✋
- 23rd in a recent A-level and GCSE league table.

Hampton School. All faiths. ✋
- 19th= in a recent A-level and GCSE league table.

Institute of Islamic Education, Dewsbury. Islamic.

The John Lyon School, London. Non-denominational.
- Founded as a day school by Harrow School.

King Edward VI School, Birmingham. All faiths. ◊ ✋
- A famous school, head of a large and unique foundation of independent and state schools in the city. 10th in a recent IB league table, 38th in a recent A-level and GCSE league table.

Kingswood House, Epsom. All faiths.

The Manchester Grammar School. All faiths. ✋
- The north of England's most famous school and one of the largest day schools in the UK. 43rd in a recent A-level and GCSE league table.

Merchant Taylors' Boys' School, Crosby. Christian.

Merchant Taylors' School, Northwood. Church of England. ✋
- One of the nine 'great public schools of England'. 40th in a recent A-level and GCSE league table.

Newcastle School for Boys. All faiths.

Queen Elizabeth Grammar School, Wakefield. All faiths.

Royal Belfast Academical Institution. All faiths.

Royal Grammar School ('RGS'), Guildford. ✋
- 37th in a recent A-level and GCSE league table.

St James Senior Boys' School, Ashford. All faiths.

Thorpe House School, Gerrards Cross. Church of England.

Victoria College, Channel Islands. Christian.

Wetherby Senior School, London. An Alpha Plus school.

Girls' day schools

Abbey School, Reading. Church of England. ✋
- 5th in a recent IB league table.

Alderly Edge School for Girls. Ecumenical. An associated school of the Woodard group.

Badminton School, Bristol. All faiths.

Bedford Girls' School. All faiths.

Blackheath High School GDST, London. All faiths.
Brighton Girls GDST. Non-denominational.
Bromley High School GDST. Non-denominational.
Bury Park Educational Institute, Luton. Islamic.
Channing School, London. Interdenominational. ✋
- 42nd in a recent A-level and GCSE league table,

City of London School for Girls. Non-denominational. ✋
- City of London Boys' School exists under the same foundation. 24th in a recent A-level and GCSE league table.

Croydon High School GDST. All faiths.
Durham High School for Girls. Church of England.
Edgbaston High School for Girls. All faiths.
Farnborough Hill. Roman Catholic.
Francis Holland School, Regent's Park, London. Church of England.
Francis Holland School, Sloane Square, London. Church of England.
Francis Holland School, Regent's Park, London. Church of England.
Godolphin & Latymer School, London. ✋
- 2nd = in a recent IB league table, 2nd in a recent A-level and GCSE league table. Very much a high-flyer.

Guildford High School. Church of England/Interdenominational. ✋
- 7th in a recent A-level and GCSE league table.

Haberdashers' Aske's School for Girls, Elstree. Christian. ✋
- 12th in a recent A-level and GCSE league table. Separate from – but associated by foundation with – Haberdashers' Aske's Boys' School.

Headington School, Oxford. Christian.
Islamiyah Girls High School, Blackburn. Islamic.
James Allen's Girls' School, London. All faiths. ✋
- 28th in a recent A-level and GCSE league table.

King Edward VI High School for Girls, Birmingham. All faiths. ✋
- 10th in a recent A-level and GCSE league table. Part of the King Edward's Birmingham group of independent and state schools.

King's High School, Warwick. Interdenominational.
The Ladies College, Guernsey. Non-denominational.
Lady Eleanor Holles School, London. All faiths. ✋
- 35th in a recent A-level and GCSE league table.

Leicester High School for Girls. Christian.
Loughborough High School. Non-denominational.

Girls' day schools

Manchester High School for Girls. Non-denominational.
The Maynard School, Exeter. Non-denominational.
- Claims to be the second-oldest girls' school in the country.

More House School, London. Roman Catholic.
Newcastle High School for Girls. Non-denominational.
North London Collegiate School. Non-denominational. ✋
- One of the earliest and most famous girls' schools, and an academic high-flyer. 2nd in a recent IB league table. 16th in a recent A-level and GCSE league table.

Northampton High School GDST. All faiths.
Northwood College for Girls GDST. All faiths.
Norwich High School GDST. All faiths.
Notre Dame Senior School, Cobham. Roman Catholic.
Notting Hill & Ealing School GDST, London. All faiths.
Nottingham Girls' High School GDST. All faiths.
Oxford High School GDST. All Faith's. ✋
- 29th in a recent A-level and GCSE league table.

Palmers Green High School, London. Non-denominational.
Pipers Corner School, High Wycombe. Church of England.
Portsmouth High School GDST. All faiths.
Putney High School GDST. All faiths. ✋
- 46th in a recent A-level and GCSE league table.

Queen's College London. Non-denominational.
Queen's Gate School, London. Non-denominational.
Redmaids' High School, Bristol. All faiths.
- Claims to be the oldest girls' school in the UK, founded in 1634.

The Queen's School, Chester. Church of England/Interdenominational.
St Alban's High School for Girls. Christian. ✋
- 33rd in a recent A-level and GCSE league table.

St Catherine's School, Twickenham. Roman Catholic.
St Helen and St Catherine's School, Abingdon. Church of England. ✋
- 41st in a recent A-level and GCSE league table.

St Helen's School, Northwood. Church of England.
St James Senior Girls' School, London. Non-denominational.
St Margaret's School for Girls, Aberdeen. All faiths.
St Mary's School, Gerrards Cross. Church of England.
St Paul's School for Girls, London. All faiths. ✋

- Separate from – but associated by foundation with – St Paul's School, which is boys-only. Academic high-flyer. 1st in a recent A-level and GCSE league table.

Sheffield High School for Girls GDST. All faiths.
Sir William Perkins School, Chertsey. Non-denominational.
Streatham & Clapham High School GDST, London. All faiths.
South Hampstead High School GDST, London. All faiths. ✋

- Top of the first-ever league table in the 1970s and a consistent high performer. 26th in a recent A-level and GCSE league table.

Surbiton High School, Kingston-upon-Thames. Church of England.
Sutton High School GDST. All faiths.
Sydenham High School GDST. All faiths.
Tormead School, Guildford. Interdenominational.
Wakefield Girls' High School. Christian.
Walthamstow Hall, Sevenoaks. All faiths.
Wimbledon High School GDST. All faiths. ✋

- 36th in a recent A-level and GCSE league table.

Withington Girls' School, Manchester. All faiths. ✋

- One of the highest-achieving girls' school in the north of England. 21st in a recent A-level and GCSE league table.

Colleges

Sixth form colleges typically educate many of their students for only one or two years – the duration of an IFP or A-level programme. As a result, there are many places available for new students each year.

While it is advisable to start looking for a college at least one year before the anticipated start date, places may be available right up to the beginning of the course. The late availability of a place at a college does not necessarily mean that it is a poor choice: it is a common situation for colleges that enrol a large number of new students each year.

There are many different types of college offering courses for overseas students, so it is important to ask questions about the particular features that you are interested in. As an example, some colleges are academically selective, meaning that they choose students with high academic test scores, obtained at their current school or in a college entry test. Some may require a high level of English proficiency. As a result of the English requirement, some colleges tend to recruit students from a small range of countries (such as Malaysia, Singapore and Hong Kong). Other colleges mostly provide IFP courses with links to middle-ranked universities. Finally, colleges can be divided into the heavily exam-focused, sometimes (if somewhat unkindly) called 'exam factories', and those that offer a more balanced approach, including extra-curricular activities. This second type of college is somewhat similar to a traditional boarding school.

The application process follows a similar pattern for most colleges. The first step is to complete an application form and send it to the college's admissions department. This form is usually available on the college's website and will ask for details of the course and subjects requested, start dates, and so on. A good college will always confirm these important details before a student joins, in order to ensure that the right academic options have been chosen for them.

The application form should be sent with copies of the student's academic record, preferably in the form of their most recent school reports. Evidence of English language proficiency is also required. This can take the form of an English exam certificate, such as the IELTS. If a student does not have such evidence, a college will provide their own English test, and this is often done online.

Many colleges will then arrange to interview the student, either face-to-face or through a video call. The interview is used to determine a student's suitability and to further assess their English language proficiency. It is also a good opportunity for a student to ask questions about the college and ensure it is the right choice for them. A good

Chapter 6 - How to Get In: Applying to a School or College

college conducts interviews using senior members of staff who can answer any questions.

As a typical example, for entry into a well-respected college for a two-year A-level programme, the student must have good grades in school exams taken around the age of 16, together with an English proficiency that is the equivalent of at least IELTS 5.5. During the interview, students must also be able to answer questions about why they wish to come to the UK and study their chosen subjects at A-level.

If a college feels that an applicant's English proficiency is too low for a particular course, such as A-level, they may offer an alternative: for instance, pre-sessional English training. This can be a good way to develop language proficiency before moving to an academic programme.

Once a student has been accepted, they are asked about their accommodation preferences for the first year. Colleges often have a range of options, including on-site or off-site boarding houses and living with a local family (homestay). The options can also include single or twin rooms, private or shared bathrooms, and self-catering or eating in the college dining room. As a result of the number of options, it is quite normal for there to be more emails about accommodation choice than about academic courses!

> **Warning:** Although college places may be available right up to a course's start date, popular accommodation (most likely on-site accommodation) is often already taken by students who enrolled earlier. It is worth booking your place early in order to have a full choice of accommodation options.

Some colleges look to attract the most able academic students by offering discounts on tuition fees, known as scholarships. A scholarship applicant may have to sit further entrance examinations (scholarship tests) and undergo a more challenging interview.

> **Warning:** Some colleges struggle to fill places, so discount their fees in order to make up a shortfall in students. In these cases, the discounts can be large. These discounts are often presented as 'scholarships' as a way of encouraging applications to less popular colleges. For this reason, do not be too strongly persuaded by a scholarship offer unless cost is an important factor.

List of independent sixth form colleges

The following list comprises colleges registered with the Independent Schools Council (ISC).

Abbey College Cambridge
Abbey College Manchester
Abbey College in Malvern
Ashbourne College, London
Bath Academy
Bellerbys College Brighton
Bellerbys College London
Bosworth Independent College, Northampton
Brampton College, London
Cambridge Tutors College, Croydon
Cardiff Sixth Form College
CATS College Cambridge
CATS College Canterbury
CATS College London
Cherwell College, Oxford
Collingham Independent College, London
Concord College, Shrewsbury
Davis, Laing and Dick College, London
d'Overbroeck's, Oxford
Ealing Independent College, London
Mander Portman Woodward Birmingham
Mander Portman Woodward Cambridge

Mander Portman Woodward London
Oxford International College
Oxford Sixth Form College
Rochester Independent College
St Andrew's College Cambridge

The best way to understand the particular features of a school or college is to visit it. This way you can tour the campus, as well as meeting the head/principal or another senior member of staff. If this isn't possible, the Covid-19 pandemic meant that many colleges (and schools) enriched their websites with much more information, including online 'tours'.

An alternative to visiting the college or school is to speak to the parents of students who have attended it, or to speak to an experienced education agent. Education agents can be very well placed to give advice about the right school for a particular student.

Warning: Many education agents offer a useful service, but they are paid by schools and colleges for each student they enrol. Some agents have preferred schools or colleges that pay them a higher commission and these may be recommended in preference to a school that could be better suited to a student's needs.

Chapter 7

How to Get In: Applying to University

The UCAS system, Choosing a course, Applications, Deciding between offers, Clearing

~

There are over 120 partly state-funded universities in the UK, and five that are entirely private. The state-funded (also known as 'public') universities include a wide range of institutions, from relatively new universities to the 800-year-old 'elite' universities of Oxford and Cambridge. The five private universities receive no funding from the government and are supported by student tuition fees.

Students apply to university using a single, standardised entry process: the Universities and Colleges Admissions Service, known as UCAS. The private universities also permit direct applications.

Students pay tuition fees to attend both public and private universities. The British government gives a partial subsidy to students from the UK who attend public universities and such students pay lower tuition fees than students from other countries.

The UCAS application system

UCAS has a tariff system that translates qualifications and grades into 'points'. Universities may demand a given number of points for entry to a course, but they do make allowances for various qualifications that do not appear on the UCAS system.

The easiest way to work out a student's points is to use the calculator on the UCAS website. The points allocated for standard UK exams are as follows:

A-level

Grade	Points
A*	56
A	48
B	40
C	32
D	24
E	16

Scottish Highers

Grade	Points
A	33
B	27
C	21
D	15

Scottish Advanced Highers

Grade	Points
A	56
B	48
C	40
D	32

International Baccalaureate (per component)

Higher Level		Standard Level	
H7	56	S7	28
H6	48	S6	24
H5	32	S5	16
H4	24	S4	12
H3	12	S3	6

	Extended Essay	Theory of Knowledge
A	12	12
B	10	10
C	8	8
D	6	6
E	4	4

Students apply to university by submitting an online UCAS application in the first term of their Year 13 studies (the second year of A-level). The application will state the five university courses that the student wishes to apply for. The five universities then independently consider the application and each decide whether or not to offer a place to that student.

University offers (or rejections) are usually made by the end of the second term of Year 13. As this is before students have sat their Year 13 exams, the university offer usually states the grades that a student must achieve in those exams. Such offers are known as 'conditional', as they depend on exam results, whether at A-level, IB or IFP.

There are rare occasions when a university makes an 'unconditional' offer. This occurs when a university is so impressed with a student that they wish them to join regardless of the results they obtain. There is pressure on universities to reduce the number of unconditional offers, as teachers report that this can affect a student's motivation and willingness to work hard after they have received such an offer.

There is continuing debate in the UK over whether or not to introduce PQA or Post-Qualification Admissions. At present most students apply before they know their actual results, and offers are made on the basis of *predicted* grades. Obviously, quite a high proportion of students will achieve either better or worse grades than predicted, which means an element of confusion on results day. Some students will fail to get the grades they need, in which case they will probably enter the Clearing Scheme (see below) to find a place. Other students will find that they have achieved better grades than expected and will seek to apply to universities with higher admission standards.

PQA would mean that offers would be made on the basis of actual grades achieved, meaning much less uncertainty in the system. At present there is no indication that PQA will be introduced, largely because of logistical and administrative obstacles.

This raises two other issues. The first is whether or not it is worthwhile cancelling a university place and re-applying elsewhere if the student gains higher grades than expected. There is no easy answer to this, and it should depend on how much the student wishes to go to the more competitive universities that their actual grades have made possible. It needs to be remembered that better grades do not guarantee a place at a better university.

Then there is the possibilitiy of a 'gap year', where the student takes a year off between school and university. Many students use this year to travel widely. Often parents are nervous about their child taking a year off, fearing that they will lose the habit of work. In practice, however, there is much to be said for a gap year. After up to 13 years of academic study, it allows the student to learn about the world independently. The student can use the gap year to build confidence and self-reliance, allowing them to start university as a more mature and resilient individual.

All this, of course, depends on how the gap year is used. If the student simply takes a year-long holiday, spending their parents' money, the advantages are much reduced. On the other hand, if the student works for six months, say, to earn money for travelling in the next six, they will learn valuable lessons about the workplace.

There are a wide variety of volunteering schemes for gap year students, which are challenging, demanding and worthwhile. A typical example is Project Trust, but there are numerous others. By and large, universities welcome the extra maturity that a gap year can bring to a student, particularly if the year has been well-used. However, a student who has not already been offered a deferred university place (a place delayed for a year) will need to remember that they might be required to attend interviews during the year, and allow for these in their plans.

Choosing a university and course

Choosing from the long list of UK universities and the even longer list of undergraduate courses can be a daunting prospect. Applicants often know the broad subject area they wish to study, such as Engineering or Business, but find that there is still a bewildering range of options to choose from. Students are strongly advised to wait until they have joined a British school before making a detailed list of university options, because they will find staff there who are experts in helping them to choose. Indeed, the availability of such advice is one of the reasons for studying at a school in the UK.

Schools and colleges are equally well placed to provide expert advice to overseas students about university options. Advice is usually given face-to-face with individual students. The process often starts many months before the application must be completed. This gives a student time to think about all of their options, to research undergraduate courses and to visit universities of interest – and, of course, to discuss the choice with their family.

When a student has narrowed down their options with the aid of their school's experts, they create their final list of five university courses. Students should ensure that they have a good first choice and a good 'insurance' choice – a lower-ranked university that will ask for lower exam grades. For example, a student may include three universities that will ask for high A-level grades (e.g. A*AA), one university that may ask for slightly less (e.g. AAB), and a fifth university that is lower still (e.g. BBB), as their insurance option. This ensures that a student will be able to enter a university where they would be happy to study, even if their final exam grades are lower than they hoped for.

> **Warning:** Some undergraduate courses require students to have taken specific subjects if they are following an A-level course (see Chapter 1). For example, a top-ranked university may ask for Maths, Further Maths and Physics for entry into an Engineering course. A lower-ranked university might ask for Maths, Physics and any other third A-level. Such subject requirements are published on university websites. Students are advised to look at those details and seek advice from their school about subject combinations, before they start their A-level course – even though they will not yet have decided exactly which university courses to apply for.

English language proficiency

In addition to specifying subject combinations and minimum A-level, IB or IFP grades, universities also require English language proficiency. There are a number of exams that assess this, but all UK universities accept the IELTS exam, and it is considered the prime qualification. Universities commonly ask for between 6.5 and 7.5, depending on the ranking of the university and the nature of the undergraduate course.

What makes a strong university application?

A strong university application must contain three features:

- It must prove that the applicant has good academic ability and strong English, both through documenting previous exam results and through Year 13 grade predictions made by the student's school.

- The application must feature a convincing Personal Statement, the short essay in which students explain their reasons for wanting to study their chosen undergraduate subject.

- The school will write a statement in support of the student, referred to as the 'reference'.

> **Warning:** A key part of the UCAS application is the personal statement. In this section the student promotes themselves to universities. While it is permissible to receive some guidance from teachers about this statement, it must be written entirely by the student and must be completely original. UCAS uses a sophisticated software programme to identify plagiarism. All applications are run through this programme and any deemed to contain work that is not original are invalidated.

Gaining a place at a top university

The UCAS system is used to apply to all state-run universities in the UK, including the most prestigious, such as Oxford and Cambridge. The usual deadline for submitting the UCAS application is 15th January of the year in which entry is sought. The deadline for Oxford, Cambridge and for applications for Medicine, Dentistry and Veterinary Medicine is earlier – the preceding 15th October. Students are not permitted to apply for both Oxford and Cambridge courses at the same time.

While the basic application process is the same for any university, the top-ranked universities have more academically able applicants than places available and this results in competition. In such cases, the way to secure an offer is by having an impressive set of academic results and predicted grades, a compelling personal statement and a supportive school reference.

In order to impress a top university, a student must provide evidence that they are a top student, for example by having a personal statement that includes a detailed description of what they have discovered about the subject they wish to study through books that they have read, visits they have made and professionals in the field to whom they have spoken.

There is a range of additional tests that students may be asked to sit when a university receives their application. For example, students applying for Medicine will be asked to sit either the BioMedical Admissions Test (BMAT) or the UK Clinical Aptitude Test (UCAT). Students applying to Oxbridge may be asked to sit a Thinking Skills Assessment (TSA). Schools and colleges often have specialist staff who help students prepare for such tests.

Before a university makes a decision about a student's application, they may require the student to attend an interview. This is a normal part of applications to Oxbridge, most Medicine courses and a number of other high-ranked universities. The process involves one or two face-to-face interviews with members of the university's admissions team and academic staff from the department the student has applied to. The interviewers are highly skilled at speaking to young people and understand how intimidating the process can be. As a result, the interview is conducted in a positive and friendly manner. Students are usually questioned about why they wish to study the subject they have applied for, the depth of their current knowledge and their ability to think about harder topics within the subject.

> **Warning:** During interviews, students are often asked questions regarding topics they have written about in their UCAS personal statement. It is therefore important to re-read the statement before the interview. Also importantly, never exaggerate your achievements or interests in your personal statement! One student who wrote down chess as an activity, but had played only once, found himself being interviewed by a chess Grand Master. Another who had put down European Film as an interest, because he thought it sounded impressive, found himself being interviewed by someone who wrote film reviews for several leading newspapers.

Choosing between university offers

After receiving decisions from all of the five universities on their UCAS application, applicants must decide which two offers to accept. A student has to choose one offer as their first choice, known as their conditional firm (or CF), and one as their second choice, known as the conditional insurance (or CI). The grades required by the university chosen as the conditional firm should be higher than those required by the insurance choice. If the student obtains grades in their final exams that are equal to or greater than their firm offer, they are then admitted into that university. If a student obtains grades that are lower than their firm offer, but still equal to or greater than their insurance offer, they are admitted into their insurance choice university.

Clearing

If a student fails to obtain the grades required for the insurance choice, or if they didn't receive offers from any of the universities they applied to, they are permitted to seek entry into other universities through a process referred to as 'clearing'. This process begins on the day when A-level results are published, in mid-August, and involves students who do not have university places being matched to universities that still have vacancies.

Although there are not usually many places available at the top universities, there will still be places at good universities. Students can often be in the confusing situation of having a number of clearing offers to choose from and are strongly advised to contact their school or college for advice. All schools in the UK will have staff ready to help students with clearing.

Chapter 8

How to Avoid a Bad School or College

Questions to ask

∼

Schools

Schools and colleges are normally judged on their results, which for most people means their league-table ranking, or on their reputation. Reputation can be problematic. If a school has a long and ancient history, it can hold on to its reputation long after it has started to underperform.

If you wonder whether a school is as good as it claims to be, here are a few things to consider.

1. What is its turnover of teaching staff?

The word 'staff' is sometimes used just to describe teachers, though strictly speaking 'staff' are all those employed by the school, ranging from the head to the cooks.

Teachers are the most important element in your child's happiness and success. If the teachers are good, the school will be good, which is why your main questions should be about the teachers.

A crucial question to ask is how many teachers leave the school each year, expressed as a percentage of the total teaching staff. Thus if there are 100 teachers in a school, and five leave every year, the 'turnover' is 5%. Teachers are probably the people who know most about a school. If large numbers of them leave every year, it can be a sign that things are going wrong.

Chapter 8 - How to Avoid a Bad School or College

As always, the prospective parent has to be careful. A staff turnover of more than 10% is a possible danger sign, but as well as asking what percentage of staff leave every year, ask why they are leaving. If it's to retirement or a more senior role, that's OK. Similarly, staff sometimes leave because their spouse or partner has moved elsewhere, or to have children or be nearer to elderly relatives. What you should look out for is teachers moving 'sideways' into another job that appears no better than the one they had previously, or teachers leaving with no job to go to. Ask two questions of the school:

- What was your staff turnover this year, as a percentage of your teaching staff?
- How many of those who left did so to take up a more senior role?

2. Were you shown round by a pupil?

If teachers know a lot about a school, the other people who know a great deal are the pupils themselves. When you're shown round, are you guided by a pupil, or at the very least given time *on your own* with a student so you can ask them what life is really like for a young person at the school? Remember that you have a right to ask any pupil questions – and be very wary of any school that seeks to stop you from talking to 'normal' pupils. You also need to bear in mind that one young person's experience of a school is not necessarily true for all students.

> **Warning:** Very often, prospective parents who visit a school do so at times when pupils should be in lessons or taking part in other activities. For this reason, it may not be possible for you to be shown round by a pupil: after all, a school that tells a child it is more important to act as a salesperson for the school than to attend a lesson could be seen as saying that marketing is more important than learning. The important thing when you are shown round a school is to take the opportunity to talk to pupils wherever possible, even if you are not shown round by one.

3. How many pupils were expelled (permanently excluded) in the last two years?

As is the case with so much of English education, there are a number of different words used for the same thing in different schools and systems. Many independent schools still use the word 'expel' when they demand that a pupil leave a school. In the state sector, and some independent schools, the word is 'exclude' or even 'suspend'. In general terms, 'expulsion' or 'permanent exclusion' means a pupil is not allowed to return to the school. 'Suspension' or 'exclusion' usually means they are not allowed to return to the school for a period of time, usually one or two weeks. Suspension or temporary exclusion are often a final warning, meaning that if a pupil misbehaves again they are likely to be expelled – but this will depend on the circumstances and the school's rules.

Every parent hopes for a school where the pupils are well-disciplined and obey the rules. If a school is expelling or excluding more than a handful of students every year, it might be a sign of major indiscipline, and of an inability to control it. Also, children do misbehave, and a school that expels or excludes pupils too easily might simply be one that does not take the time and trouble to find out why a child is misbehaving and seek to help them.

4. Drugs and sex

Most parents will not feel happy asking a school if it expels or excludes pupils found taking drugs. They will worry about the school assuming that their child is a drug user, and thus not offering them a place. It is also true that many parents are attracted by 'zero tolerance' attitudes to drug usage, whereby the school states that any involvement with drugs will result in a pupil losing their place at the school.

Parents think that the fear of being expelled will encourage pupils not to take drugs. Unfortunately, this is not always true. Young people can be risk-takers, and the severity of the penalty makes the activity exciting. Remember also that many young people experiment with drugs either to boost their image among their peer group, or to avoid being laughed at as cowards. It is a sad fact that when young people are caught taking drugs in school such as cannabis or LSD, it is often the relatively innocent, first-time users who are caught, not the regular users or the dealers.

For this reason, many schools will punish first-offence drug usage, but not expel for it, insisting instead that a pupil found taking drugs is subject to random drug-testing and expelled if he or she re-offends. The advantage of this system is that it creates a socially acceptable reason for the pupil to say no, and one which brings no shame among their peer group: the pupil can point to the fact that if he or she takes drugs, they are likely to be found out and expelled.

Some schools have zero-tolerance or one-strike-and-you're-out policies for sexual relationships, which in some cases can be as unjust and unfair as similar policies with regard to drugs. On the other hand, many schools have more nuanced ways of navigating these issues, which are worth parents enquiring about.

There is no universal guide to this issue, only questions to ask each individual school. These might include:

- What happens if my child finds a boyfriend or girlfriend while at school?

- What policies and processes protect children from non-consensual sexual conduct?

- What policies govern the school's treatment of these matters?

There has been major controversy in the UK over issues of sexual harassment by school-age young people, focussing mainly on bad behaviour by boys to girls. One result of this is that many schools now have robust policies and strategies for dealing with these issues.

No head or principal will be surprised or offended if you raise questions about their policies on sexual relationships or drugs, and they should be able to give you a full account of how the school deals with all aspects of these issues.

Remember that a bad school is one that simply gets rid of pupils who misbehave. A good school is more humane, and teaches students to behave better.

5. How long will the head teacher stay for?

A good head or principal is crucial to a school's success. When a parent meets a head they like and who is clearly doing a good job, they often ask, 'How long are you staying as Head?' In other words, the parent wants to know whether the head teacher they are meeting will be the same one who guides their child through school.

It is actually a useless question to ask. No head will ever tell a parent if they are applying for other jobs, partly because for it to be known would undermine their authority, and partly because if a job application fails, few people want others to know!

If there is no point in asking how long a head is staying, there is every point in looking to see how many heads the school has had in the past 10 years. As a very rough guide, you might expect a head to stay for at least five years, or the time it takes to see a generation of new pupils through the school. Anything earlier might be completely innocent – a recruiting consultant could have rung unexpectedly and asked the head to apply for one of the very top schools – or it could suggest a school that is in trouble, or that its governing body cannot sustain a working relationship with its head.

6. Look for detail

Many schools have invested millions of pounds in facilities. Do not be fooled by the lovely sports hall or theatre. In order to pay for the building and its upkeep, some schools have to hire it out to the local community. Can your son or daughter go to the sports hall or swimming pool in the evening or at weekends, or will it have been hired out to paying customers?

However, the buildings are less important than the humans who work in them. When you go round a school, look to see whether the site is clear from litter. Notice whether there are weeds growing beneath the paving slabs. Look to see if paint is lifting off the window frames. If the school does not take pride in the appearance of its buildings and grounds, is it going to take pride in the education of your child?

7. Weekends

A bad school will leave its boarding pupils to their own devices at weekends – and for a child thousands of miles away from home, family and friends, weekends can be a very lonely time. Ask how many boarders stay at the school over the weekend, if this is what your child will need to do, and what arrangements are made for them.

Also ask whether there are weekends when the school is closed, and what help the school will give to accommodate your child when this happens.

Some schools will claim that a high percentage of their students are 'full boarders', present at the school for the whole of term time. In fact, an increasing number of schools who claim 'full boarding' actually release pupils at weekends. It is not hard to understand why. Parents who choose to send their children to boarding schools often live relatively nearby, perhaps not more than an hour's travelling time. If they come over to see their child play in a sports fixture on a Saturday afternoon, or perform in a concert or play on a Saturday evening, it is natural to want to take them home for the night and bring them back to school as late as possible on Sunday evening.

However, it is not always a bad thing if overseas students are the majority of those present at weekends. It can allow these students to form close friendships and develop a team spirit.

> **Warning:** Sunday is a special day of the week for Christians. Traditionally it was the 'day of rest', and for much of the history of the UK no work was permitted on Sundays (for example, all shops were closed) and people's sole responsibility was to attend a church service. Much of this has changed in modern Britain: only 5% of the population regularly attend a Christian religious service. Nonetheless, schools do not teach on Sundays, and many of their staff will not be at work. For this reason, when choosing a school or college, ask what your child will do on a Sunday.

There is little point in travelling thousands of miles to go to school unless the child can learn at least a little about British culture and history. Schools do not always feel they have to organise trips to London, to Cambridge or to Stratford-upon-Avon (the birthplace of William Shakespeare) for their British pupils. Ask them whether arrangements will be made for overseas pupils to be exposed to the immensely rich culture and history of the UK.

This is particularly important for boarding schools, because many are situated in relatively isolated, rural areas. This can make them somewhat inward-looking, teaching children how to live in and adapt to the school's own culture, but barely exposing them to wider British and European society.

8. Opportunity for all

Every school a parent looks at will have its 1st XI soccer and cricket teams, its 1st XV for rugby, and its orchestra. The problem is that not every child who loves soccer is very good at it! In all the areas your child might be interested in – drama, music and sport are common examples – ask what opportunities there are for the child who is enthusiastic but perhaps not particularly skilled. In many boarding schools, the house system copes admirably with this problem. As well as school teams and plays, there are house competitions for sport and music, and this can expand to include house plays and even art competitions.

9. Subject results

Always ask to see a school's examination results divided up by subject. Expect to see not just the most recent results but the results for the previous year as well. Why is this so important? Schools can be excellent in some subjects, but rubbish in others. There is a shortage of good teachers in the UK as there is in almost every country in the world, and subjects for which it is notoriously difficult to get good teachers include Economics, Mathematics, Physics and Chemistry. Check the school's results against the subject your son or daughter wants to take: these are the results that matter to you, and to them.

10. Destinations

One of the main reasons why we send our children to school is to allow them to pursue a rewarding career. In most cases the overseas student will come to the UK in the first place because they want to gain a place at a top university, be that in the UK, Europe or the USA. Ask to see the destinations of all leavers for at least the past two years. Are they taking top courses at top universities? Or are they going to universities with low entrance standards, reducing the likelihood of a good career afterwards?

11. Professional organisations

There are a number of professional organisations to which most independent schools belong. The best-known are the HMC (Headmasters' and Headmistresses' Conference) and GSA (Girls' Schools Association), but there are a significant number of others, most of which are joined under the umbrella of the ISC (Independent Schools Council), the organisation representing most independent schools.

Membership of the HMC, GSA and other organisations tells parents something about the quality of a school, because all these organisations have standards that schools have to meet before they are allowed membership. Parents don't need to look out so much for *which* organisation the school is a member of, but for whether or not it is a member of *any* organisation. A school that is not affiliated to a professional organisation may or may not be a rogue school, but it is certainly something to investigate further. The worst-case scenario is often when a school has been expelled from a professional organisation. You need to know why, if this is the case.

> **Warning:** Usually the professional organisations representing fee-paying schools have no power to discipline a school for bad behaviour. Their only power is to take away a school's membership. Therefore, there is little point in complaining to one of the professional organisations if you feel that you have been badly served by a school. This does not, of course, remove your legal rights, nor your right to complain to the Department for Education if you think that serious or illegal misconduct has taken place.

12. Culling

A practice that may still be found in some schools and colleges is

Chapter 8 - How to Avoid a Bad School or College

the forced removal of a pupil who is not likely to gain a top grade at GCSE or A-level, thereby lowering the school or college's league table ranking. This is sometimes known as a school 'culling' its students. In most cases this will apply to a younger pupil wishing to enter the sixth form for A-level or IB, but it can apply in exceptional circumstances to a pupil finishing their first year of A-level studies and wishing to continue into the final year.

There is an important distinction here, however. Sometimes a school might appear to be culling a student, when in fact what they are doing is perfectly justifiable. This arises when a pupil, after their first year of A-level or IB study is clearly not, with their current progress, going to obtain the grades they need to get into their chosen university. Even with excellent teaching, this can still happen for a number of reasons. Perhaps the young person's English has held them back; perhaps they did not cover vital parts of the

A-level or IB specification in their home country; perhaps it has taken them time to settle into the school. In any event, the school might well suggest that they repeat a year and delay sitting their final examinations. This is likely to be unwelcome news for both the parent and the child, but it is often good advice. If a pupil desperate to study Medicine gets a C and two Ds at A-level, they won't get a place at university, and that rejection will be on their record for ever.

There is a very real difference between this and the school not allowing someone to progress because they fear that the school, rather than the pupil, will be harmed by poor results. To guard against the latter, undesirable policy, simply ask the school or college whether they require a minimum level of achievement before a pupil is allowed to progress from one year to the next.

Colleges

Most of the important features of schools are also found in colleges, which means that many of the questions to be asked when choosing a school apply equally well. For example, a high turnover of staff in either a school or college may indicate the same thing – unhappy teachers and a poor environment in which to be a student.

Because colleges specialise in the final stages of pre-university education and often have a diverse and international student body, there are further questions you may wish to consider.

1. What kind of college is it?

There is a lot of variety in how colleges see their purpose, as well as in how they act. At one extreme are the so-called 'exam factory' colleges, which solely emphasise exam results and have a very narrow offering for sport, music and other extra-curricular activities. The facilities at such colleges may be limited to areas for academic study, such as classrooms and laboratories. They may not have a sports hall or outside play space.

Other colleges see their role as being to help students not just with their final exam results but also with their personal development as they move into adulthood. Such colleges will have a wider range of facilities, more like a school's.

It is worth noting that universities expect students to have interests beyond the classroom. If you choose an 'exam factory' style college, it is still important that a student can demonstrate interests beyond their schoolwork.

2. Boarding

Colleges differ in their approach to boarding overseas students. This is discussed in Chapter 3. Some colleges have boarding houses close to the main teaching site, or even on-site, where highly qualified and experienced staff care for the students. At the other extreme, colleges may have few boarding staff, who may not be as well trained in caring for students – or no boarding facilities at all. It is worth asking how a college ensures the safety and wellbeing of its boarding students. For example, you may look for a college that has its own dedicated healthcare provision.

3. Are staff trained in teaching overseas students?

Academic study in English is a challenge for all students who do not have English as their first language. While there are new words that all students must learn for particular subjects ('subject-specific vocabulary' or 'jargon'), overseas students must also understand their teacher's spoken delivery, as well as course textbooks that are designed for fluent speakers of English. This challenge is often the single most significant barrier to academic success. An important question to ask, therefore, is to what extent the teachers in a college are aware of this barrier and are trained in how to overcome it.

4. Does the college understand the cultural background of overseas students?

It is not uncommon to hear teachers say that they find some overseas students to be reserved and 'shy' and report that they have difficulty in eliciting classroom participation from them. The reality is that such teachers have not been sufficiently well prepared and trained in the cultural differences between British students and some of those from overseas. This can result in confusion and upset when overseas students feel exposed and isolated in lessons taught by teachers who do not appreciate the different learning culture and expectations such students have grown up with. A good college will ensure that its teachers are trained in understanding these differences and sympathetic to the different backgrounds of overseas students.

5. How well do students from different backgrounds mix?

Colleges are justifiably popular with overseas families, and as a result their student bodies can contain significant numbers of foreign students. Some colleges will have a history of recruiting from a particular country and this can mean that many students may come from one place and speak the same language. Some parents worry that their children will therefore only spend their time with other children from their home country.

A key question to ask the college is how it encourages students to make friends from different backgrounds. A good college will have a deliberate and well-considered approach to this. When done well, it gives the child the wonderful experience of learning about other cultures and countries. Such children will also have the beginnings of a network of future social or business contacts across the globe.

6. What happens if my child falls behind academically? Will they be expelled?

The academic programmes taken by overseas students in UK colleges are demanding. Bear in mind that the 'A' in 'A-level' is short for 'Advanced', which indicates the high academic level required for success. It is to be expected that some students will struggle at times during such demanding programmes, especially as they are delivered in English.

Ask what is done in a college to track students' academic performance and what is done if they fall behind. Some colleges may have weak systems to identify academic problems and may not offer additional support for underperforming students. It is also important to establish whether a college expels students for poor academic performance (see point 12 in the list for schools, above). Ask a college whether this is their practice and, if so, what grades are required in order to progress to the second year of A-level.

7. Can you show me a complete set of results and university destinations for the past few years?

It is worth asking for a breakdown of the full set of academic results from a college, in detail, for a number of years. A good college will be completely open about students' results for all past years and will publish them in full on their website. On the other hand, some colleges may be content to highlight the performance of a carefully chosen number of top students. If that is the case, ask about the performance of all students in order to see a balanced picture.

Chapter 9

What Makes an Excellent School or College?

Wellbeing, Extra-curricular activities, Culture, University preparation

∼

Schools

Much of what makes a good school has been covered in the preceding chapters, and of course many of the things that make a good school also make a good college. However, there are particular marks of quality that you should look out for and ask about.

The most important thing is to realise that you have the right to ask questions. Most of us were taught as children to respect our teachers and our school, and to accept their authority. However, to ask questions of your child's future school is not to disrespect it: rather, this will be expected.

It is the same as buying any other product. Although this 'product' is more expensive and more personal than many others you will buy, you still need to check it out and reassure yourself that it does what it claims to. In doing so, you demonstrate that you care.

Mental health and wellbeing (pastoral care)

The testimonial from a Brighton College student in the next chapter proves an important point: the academic or intellectual content on offer at a school is hugely important, but unless the emotional environment is good, a child will not succeed there. Young people need to feel good about themselves: confident and well cared for. This is an area where British education can sometimes succeed very well, just as it sometimes helps children to obtain outstanding results.

Young people across the world report being under increased pressure to succeed. That pressure is even greater on overseas students, whose parents have often made financial sacrifices in order to send them to the UK. A happy student is a successful student, but every young person, wherever they come from, will face times of strain and stress: be it over worry that they will not pass examinations, that they are not making friends or, for overseas students, that they are losing contact with their family and relations back home.

A recent paper issued by the UK government suggested that every school in the UK should have a Designated Lead for Mental Health and Wellbeing, meaning a teacher whose job is to ensure that a child or student with worries or causes of unhappiness receives the necessary help or support. Your chosen school should have such a person.

You will *not* reduce your child's chances of gaining a place at a top school or college by asking about their systems for ensuring pupil wellbeing and happiness. Instead, this will show that you are a caring parent, and schools want parents who care about their children and do not take their wellbeing for granted.

Remember the words of a leading headmaster: *If I were choosing a school for one of my own children, I would not wish to know how the school performed when everything was going well. Any school can do that. I would want to know that the school still wanted to care for and love my child every bit as much when things go wrong as when things are going well.*

What happens outside the classroom can have as much of an effect on your child's success as what happens inside it. At the same time, it's important to recognise that things will not go well all the time for even the best student, and there will be times when they are unhappy or upset. Ask what arrangements your chosen school has in place to monitor the wellbeing of students, and what help they can offer if the student is unhappy.

Music

All schools will have orchestras, choirs and other musical groups. However, you may need to ask whether your child can get into them! For example, if your child is an enthusiastic musician but has not been studying their instrument for very long, they might not qualify for the school orchestra. Are there training groups that a student can join, which will prepare them for joining the main orchestra later?

For a skilled musician, the key is often the number of public performances with an audience that the school can offer on a regular basis. Some schools go so far as to guarantee their top musicians a performance in front of an audience every fortnight.

In other words, if music is an interest, you should ask what programme the school has for a student at your child's skill level. The best school orchestra in the country is no use to your child if they cannot get into it!

Finally, it's worth noting that different schools have different musical strengths. If you look at three very musical schools, you may find that one has a famous choir, one has a marching band that travels the world, while the third is particularly strong in jazz performance and pop music production.

Here are some questions to ask:

- What opportunities are there for my child to get better at playing their instrument or singing?
- What opportunities will there be for my child to win a place in an orchestra or choir?

- What opportunities will my child have to perform in front of an audience?

Sport

Many schools are rightly proud of their sporting provision. Sport is not just enjoyable: the training and perseverance it requires are as good for the mind as for the body. It teaches people to challenge themselves and to be members of a team; how to win, but also how to cope with losing. These are crucial skills for the workplace, as well as for university.

However, an international student does not always get the best sporting opportunities. Firstly, with some overseas schools not having large playing fields, many students arrive in the UK having had little or no experience of playing soccer, rugby or a number of other team sports – and usually no experience at all of playing cricket! This can put them at a disadvantage compared to British students, many of whom will have been playing these sports for years, and often since early childhood.

Also, a student entering the sixth form for a two-year A-level or IB course will be joining a group of students who have already been at the school for three or five years, who have played in junior teams, and who expect to be in the 1st XI or 1st XV[*] when they become senior students. People can react negatively if they lose their place in the squad to a newly arrived student.

It's worth asking these questions:

- Are there opportunities for my son or daughter to *learn* to play the various sports on offer at the school?

---

[*] Rather confusingly, British schools use roman numerals when referring to the number of players in a team. Thus the first (or top) team in soccer is known as the 1st XI, 'XI' being the roman numeral for '11', because there are 11 players in a soccer team, while the top team in rugby, containing 15 players, is known as the 1st XV, 'XV' being the roman numeral for '15'.

- As a new arrival, will my son or daughter be allowed to play in the top teams if they are good enough?

Culture, history and current affairs

If you are sending your child to the UK, it's likely that the aim is to prepare them for a British or American university. It therefore makes sense if, while here, they have the chance to learn a little about both cultures. It's been said that Britain and America are two countries divided by (almost) the same language. You can see the truth of this in things as different as university culture on the one hand, and spellings and the meanings of words on the other. In the UK, if you want to look at the engine of a car you lift the *bonnet*. In the USA, you lift the *hood*. If you walk into a shop and ask where you can buy *pants*, in the UK you will be sent to the department that sells *underwear*, whereas in America, you will be sent to the department that sells *trousers*. In the UK, a student studies *Maths*. In the USA they study *Math*. There is no need for the student to know about or learn these differences before they come to the UK, but it is a good idea for them to know that such differences exist.

Learning about British and/or American culture has decided advantages when it comes to applying to university. It not only shows respect on the part of the student, but suggests that they take an interest in their surroundings and know how to adapt. An boy who was asked at an interview for the University of Cambridge, 'Why do you think there are so many churches in Cambridge?' did not recommend himself when he answered, 'I didn't notice many churches'. The answer suggested that he was not observant or curious.

A second reason for asking whether a school has a cultural programme is simply that learning about foreign societies is important in the modern world. If either of the authors of this book sent their children or grandchildren overseas to study, they would expect them to learn about the culture of the country in which they were being educated.

Cultural education can take many forms, including trips to museums, art galleries and historical sites, and even to the theatre. The government insists that schools include 'British values' in what they teach, and good schools will have adapted this requirement so that they offer something culturally informative to overseas students. Schools that prepare students for universities in the USA will run courses not just on SATs and how to get into an Ivy League university, but on American culture in general. Learning about another country's culture does not mean that your identity is absorbed by it, but simply that you come to understand and respect it.

Through the act of applying to an overseas university, a student states that they wish, in a sense, to be a global citizen. In doing so, they will create the expectation that they know what is happening in the world. They should keep abreast of current affairs and read a newspaper, in print or online, every day. A student with an enquiring mind will want to know what is happening in the world around them, and universities and employers want young people with enquiring minds. Such a person will be impressive at interview.

The home culture and language of the student

If a student should be able to learn about European and American culture, it is also true that the overseas student should be at an institution that respects his or her own culture. For example, will an overseas student who is interested in calligraphy have support to improve their ability in their new school? Similarly, there are often wonderful opportunities to learn new sports in the UK, particularly team sports. But what about sports that the student is already familiar with? A good school will provide the opportunity to learn new sports, but it should also allow the student to carry on playing table tennis or basketball, to name two examples.

Another question, already discussed in this book, is whether the student will have access to a teacher or adult employed by the school or college who speaks their own language. Of course an overseas student comes to the UK to improve their English, and of course a good school will discourage a student from speaking only their native language. On the other hand, there will be times when a student needs to express themselves in their own language, and perhaps have it translated.

One example might be if a student worries after a few weeks that they have chosen the wrong A-level subject. This is a complicated issue. Is it because the student is genuinely not suited to the subject in question, or is it because there are gaps in their pre-existing knowledge? Is it because they do not like their teacher? It is vital that the school finds out exactly what is going on, and it is entirely possible that even the best student's command of English might not be advanced enough to let the school get to the bottom of the problem.

Emotional issues can also make access to a home-language speaker important. If a student is feeling homesick or is worried about the health of a relative, they often need the comfort and familiarity of their own language if they are to discuss it properly.

Another useful addition can be a language specialist to liaise and communicate with parents, whose command of English is often weaker than that of their children.

Reading

Students' spoken skills often advance more rapidly than their written English. A good school will encourage overseas students to read books and articles in English. These should not just be academic materials, and they should include things that students will enjoy reading.

Chapter 9 - What Makes an Excellent School or College?

Not only will this reading enhance the student's learning of English: it will also impress universities. We cannot emphasise too strongly the advantage to a student when their university application demonstrates *intellectual curiosity*: the desire to know more than they have been taught. They should want not just to repeat other people's knowledge, but to increase their own.

Work/study skills

Schools everywhere can sometimes make the process of learning too easy for the student, telling them exactly what to do and when. However, by the time a student reaches A-level or the IB, it is rarely that simple. They will often be given an assignment and told when it needs to be handed in, but not when or how to do it. A student taking three A-levels, alongside English language lessons, may have four or five assignments to work on at once. They will have to plan carefully to make sure that all are handed in on time – just like a chef cooking five different foods, who must bring them to the table together.

Knowing how to plan and timetable your independent work is part of what is known in the UK as 'study skills'. Study skills are not about *what* work you do, but about *how* you do it. Other skills looked at under this heading including taking notes from lectures or lessons or from books – essential for those hoping to go to university.

Good schools help their students to develop effective study skills. If a school doesn't, ask them why.

Olympiads

There are national and international competitions in a number of subjects (mainly Maths and the sciences), known as Olympiads, where students compete against each other for gold, silver or bronze medals. These Olympiads are excellent events, offering significant benefits for the young people who take part. They challenge students to know and do more, and tend to improve the knowledge and study skills of everybody who takes part. Meanwhile, those who win medals demonstrate that they are star students: they have proved themselves on a national or global stage.

- Does your chosen school enter pupils for international Olympiads? If not, why not?

Leadership, responsibility, civic duty

One of the greatest schools in the world, the Raffles Institution in Singapore, offers the Raffles Diploma alongside its A-level course. To receive a Diploma, students have to reach a high standard in five areas, of which academic achievement (Cognitive Skills) is only one. The other four areas are Character & Leadership, Community and Citizenship, Sports & Health, and Arts and Aesthetics. All of these are important, and not only because they help the student develop into a rounded and mature adult.

If a student has these skills and attributes, it marks them out. Parents of high-achieving children, and indeed the children themselves, sometimes think that gaining top marks is all it takes to get a place at a top university. They forget that the world's top universities will have five or more applicants for each place, almost all of whom are likely to have top grades. How do you choose between five students when you only have one place to offer and all of them have A* grades? Will you give the place to the student who has simply done their work and succeeded at it, or will you give it to the student who as well as working hard and gaining top grades has been a glowing example to their peer group, shown themselves a leader, given back to their local community, and excelled in sport or music?

Universities themselves realise that their students will not study 24 hours per day. They will have a social life, and they will do other activities. A sensible university does not just look to see whether a student works hard, but also whether they can continue to work hard when they are playing hard. Remember that a university is not just interested in how well a student has done in the past: they want to know how well they will do in the future.

Schools in the UK do not offer the Raffles Diploma, though some do have their own equivalents. Parents should make sure that their chosen school gives the overseas boy or girl opportunities to show leadership and to develop their character, to become involved in community work and learn to help others, to engage in sport and understand how to live healthily, and to appreciate and, if they have the skills, participate in art, music and drama.

University preparation

This important area is discussed below: the same considerations apply to both schools and colleges.

Colleges

A global community

Most UK colleges have a diverse range of nationalities in their student body. This can result in an enriching experience for young people as they make friends from all over the world, discovering cultural similarities and differences. Students also begin to learn that the things uniting people are far greater than those that divide them: they see that their new friends often have the same dreams that they do. This can be useful in their later careers, if they work in areas such as business or science that involve international cooperation.

A good college fully embraces this culture and works to foster a strong feeling of community between students, regardless of their home country. One approach is to form students into mixed groupings through the use of a 'house' system. This fosters mixed-group identities within the college and encourages students to work, engage in competition and play sport with other students, often from different countries, within their house. Another common approach is to insist that only English is used by students in lessons and college activities. This prevents students from feeling isolated by a conversation in a language they don't understand, while also promoting English language skills.

A learning culture

A high turnover of teaching staff can indicate dissatisfaction within a teaching body and result in a poor college, just as it can in a school (see Chapter 8). The best colleges have a stable and engaged teaching staff who themselves enjoy learning, which creates a learning culture that inspires students. This may take the form of teachers forming study groups to read about and discuss important areas of education, such as the science of teaching, or how to influence student motivation. Other approaches include teachers observing their colleagues at work, then discussing and comparing their practices.

Progress is monitored and action is taken

Most students at UK colleges are undertaking short, one or two-year academic programmes, so any difficulties must be identified and acted on quickly. Best practice involves a student having regular meetings, often shared with a few other children, with a member of staff who is tasked with overseeing their progress. This staff member is often referred to as a 'personal tutor'. Daily tutor meetings can result in a student feeling cared for and able to admit areas of concern. Regular testing also reveals the gaps in a student's knowledge and can be used to target interventions such as one-to-one teaching sessions.

The 'personal tutor' system is useful in schools, as well as colleges.

University preparation

A key reason for choosing a sixth form college is the emphasis placed on the next stage – university. A good college will understand what is required for a strong university application, as well as the particular challenges faced by overseas students.

The best university preparation programmes do not rely on students researching courses by themselves, but instead teach them how to do it, through a detailed, structured course of reading, presentations and visits to university departments. Such programmes may even start before the student arrives at the college, providing a reading list in the summer before the course starts. Visiting speakers who have expertise in popular fields (for example, engineering), can be particularly inspiring. Former students who entered a top university may be invited back to the college to share their experiences and offer advice.

The British education system places great value on critical thinking and on students developing and defending their own views. Teaching staff at a good college work continuously to help students develop these traits and are keenly aware that these can be new and difficult things for some overseas students.

An effective approach is the use of one-to-one interviews with a college teacher. In such interviews, students are asked to speak in depth about their chosen subject and have to create and defend arguments and give views about news stories or recent developments. They are challenged with questions such as 'Why do you think that?', 'How else could you solve this problem?' and 'Now give me the opposite side of the argument.'

Chapter 10

A Day in the Life of ...

Two sixth form students at Abbey College, Cambridge

After a hearty breakfast I would head to my tutor's classroom for a five-minute group meeting before lessons started. We would chat about the news and our studies, and there would sometimes even be time for a quick debate or presentation.

I took Mathematics, Further Mathematics, Chemistry and Physics, with four hours for each subject every week. Because I had been learning English for a long time, I only needed two weekly English lessons to attain a satisfactory level.

Physics and Chemistry had a practical aspect. We would design our own experiments and write reports on them. The complexity of these experiments was varied. Sometimes we would just drop balls on a pressure plate, with the aim of determining the earth's gravitational acceleration, while at other times it would be a two hours of organic synthesis! My Chemistry teacher was particularly meticulous with our report grading. I learned many useful tips from him.

Once lessons were over, I would head to a club. My interests were varied, and I was a member of the philosophy and astronomy clubs. I even created my own chemistry club, where I would teach university level chemistry to fellow students. At other times I would take part in circuit training or swimming.

On Thursdays, lessons would finish early, at around 2pm, because afterwards Year 12 students would have Pre-Degree Diploma lessons on a subject of their choice. I was in a team working on an engineering project, and an ARM engineer would come over to help. We would also meet at weekends to discuss the project's next steps.

After dinner I would head to the library, where I would review the day's topics and practise for science competitions – always with an eye on the International Chemistry Olympiad.

Agustin

Every day that I am at Abbey College I strive to improve myself. I always look forward to any clubs that challenge me: I find them very enjoyable. These are held by students and teachers who are dedicated to working harder because they have a burning passion.

These clubs allow me to keep engaged with Olympiads and with my A-Level subjects: Maths, Physics and Chemistry. I also aim to keep a balance between my social life, my health and my academic development, within the constraints of my timetable!

Juan Francisco

A GCSE student at Abbey College

As GCSE students, not only do we go over the topics listed on the specification, but we are also encouraged to go beyond the course and into more advanced topics to get a taste of what it is that we want to study in the future. This is complemented by weekly 'Abbey Inspires' sessions, to enrich our knowledge and widen our perspective, as well as extra-curricular clubs which are led by teachers or keen students.

Victoria

A junior boarding pupil at Brighton College

I landed at Heathrow. It was a gloomy day in Britain, but I found this strangely calming. Everyone was quiet, getting along with their business, walking through the airport at a steady pace. I had been told by relatives and friends that I should feel excited or scared, happy or sad, as I approached my new life. Yet all I felt was weird, as if I was watching myself from the outside. I was so deep in my thoughts that when the customs officer asked me what I was doing here in the UK, I blurted out my name instead.

The next thing I knew, I was at school and saying goodbye to Mum. I saw people crying as their parents left, but I didn't. There was no point, when I would see her in a month or two. But perhaps what stopped me was the grip of toxic masculinity, reaching out to me from my previous school.

I am often asked the reason why I chose to leave my hometown for the UK. I know people want me to say that I left in pursuit of a better education, so I say that, to stop them pressing for an answer.

I left my old school for deeper reasons. Students there were ranked at the end of the year, and this determined their classes for the next. There were nine classes in total. Not only did their rank influence people's self-worth, it also affected the quality of teaching that they received and the school's attitude towards them. Though I ranked near the top of my year, I felt uneasy about the situation. I knew I would be seen differently if I dared to underperform in my end-of-year exams. The longer I stayed there, the more I realised that students were merely numbers on an Excel sheet.

On top of that came the bullying. I was not the target of bullying, but seeing others being bullied and not speaking up for them was the worst feeling I've ever had. Even worse was seeing those who dared report incidents to teachers be dismissed with the phrase 'boys will be boys', and then becoming the victims of bullying themselves.

Chapter 10 - A Day in the Life of ...

I immediately felt safe at Brighton College, with a new identity and a past that no one knew about. The question was, with this blank slate, how should I present myself to others? Who did I want to be, and how should I go about re-inventing myself? I did not have any answers.

Then came the next day, my first actual school day at Brighton College. It was 7 a.m. and I woke up with a massive headache, probably because of the thinking I had done during the night. I stumbled down to the common room of my boarding house. People seemed busy, purposeful, walking in and out of rooms and up and down the corridors, creating a commotion. For once in my life, I was at a complete loss. Fear and confusion hit me like a tsunami, but I knew better than to show these emotions, especially in front of my new tutor group. I took a deep breath and before I knew it, I was in Chapel.

Though I'm not particularly religious, there is something pleasant about the chapel in my school: something refreshingly calm. Gone were the screeching sounds of confusion. All I knew at that moment was stillness, with everyone reflecting alongside me, and I felt less alone.

Suddenly the organ stopped and the headmaster stepped onto the podium.

As expected, we were given the 'Welcome to Brighton College' speech. 'Kindness,' he said, 'kindness is what bonds us all in this school. Those who don't believe in kindness have no place in this institution.' I had heard of ambition in a beginning of year speech. I'd also heard of hard work, tenacity, grades and discipline, but kindness was new. Frankly, my previous school and kindness were like oxymorons – simply incompatible. Instead of simply telling us to 'be better', my new headmaster told us to be ourselves. The last thing I remember about his speech is that he told us to be 'the best versions of ourselves, not a second-rate version of someone else'.

People often lose sight of what they can become when they fixate on what they are in this time and place. Instead of creating an artificial version of myself, I figured that it was more important to discover who I was and live authentically. My headmaster's advice played a large part in how I made peace with myself and came to own my identity, unashamedly. The UK can be cold and humid – in short, the weather is often unpleasant – but it is the kindness in my school that keeps me going. It keeps me going today as much as it kept me going in my early days studying abroad. I may have lost myself in my old school, but I found myself again at Brighton College.

Anonymous

Conclusion

Good luck in your search for a school or college!

We, the authors of this book, are two very fortunate people, because we have witnessed at first hand the intelligence, drive and creativity that overseas students bring to UK schools and colleges. Of course, we would like this book to sell well. What author doesn't? But we can't emphasise too strongly that we have not written it for commercial reasons. Much more importantly, we feel that parents who send their children to a foreign country to further their education and enhance their prospects in life deserve the best impartial advice.

The pages above contain warnings about many potential problems. However, bear in mind that the great majority of overseas students who come to the UK find it a wholly rewarding experience – and in many cases, one that sets them up for their life ahead.

We wish you and your children every possible success.

Dr Julian Davies
Dr Martin Stephen